PARLANDO II

This book is dedicated
to
Nina, Lance, Diane and Scott, and Anuška

Ray Clark Dickson is father of the new West Coast poetry—sings like Blake, burns like Bukowski. RCD does blue-collar and white-collar poetry in the same laundry. He follows readings here by Derek Walcott and Norman Mailer.

—D.G. Wills, D.G. Wills Books, La Jolla, California

Kevin Clark, Ph.D, Professor of English, a major Poet-in-Residence, Cal Poly, SLO, wrote the three-page foreword to Ray's *Parlando* (295 poems, 295 pages retrospective, first printing sold out in Edinburgh and U.K. distribution centers). The following is an excerpt:

Most of RCD's formal energy derives from the brilliant jazz-blown waves of participial phrasing. Over and over again, a prepositional phrase is risen out of stasis by gerund. In the clickety-click ching of his lines, he delivers the adrenalinic music of the centurys' explorers who went off for story and returned with poems, then went off again. Dickson's poems insist that, searched well, the world has many astonishing and sustaining beauties—human, aural, kinetic. And the poems also insist that the inquisitive, fraternal drive toward the next day is probably the world's most alluring beauty. To open these pages is to begin that drive.

PARLANDO II

Selected Poems

Ray Clark Dickson

Publications, Partial

Art-life; Askew; Art-Rag; Beloit Poetry Journal; Bitterroot; Bouillabaisse; Café Solo; Solo I; Caprice; Clark Street Revue; Coffeehouse Poets Quarterly; Earth Words; IO; KC Press; Kinesis (narrative poetry prize); *Mandrake Poetry Magazine* (Gliwice, Poland); *Pembroke Magazine; New Times,* San Luis Obispo; *Northcoast View; Northwest Revue; Old Crow; Red Hen Press; River Rat Revue; Saturday Evening Post; Southwest Regional Magazine; The 2010-11 San Diego Poetry Annual; The Benicia Herald; The Haight-Ashbury Literary Journal; The Kerouac Connection; The Portland Oregonian; The San Luis Obispo Tribune; The Smith; Sure; The Tomcat; Toyon; White Crow Press; Wormwood Revue; Yellow Silk Revue, Crown Publishers, NYC.*

Poems have also appeared in chapbooks, *Be A Good Guy And Play Your Guitar Sweetly; Behind The Blue-Velvet Curtain; San Diego Suite: Impressions In Prose Of A City; The Last Whale; The San Francisco Pit Band Blues;* U.C.L.A.'s Special Collection Poetry Archives.

In the anthology *A Fine Excess: Fifty years of the Beloit Poetry Journal,* the author was honored to be beside Langston Hughes, whose translation of Lorca's *Gypsy Ballads* became available for the first time. Selections were from 1200 entrants published since 1950.

Available in Bookstores:
Ninth book: iUniverse, *The Press Corps Of Xanadu*
Tenth book: Red Hen Press, Los Angeles, CA,
       Wingbeats After Dark
Eleventh Book: **Infinity Publishing**, West Conshohocken, PA,
With The Blood of Butterflies

PARLANDO II

Selected Poems

Ray Clark Dickson

PARLANDO II
SELECTED POEMS

iUniverse books may be ordered through booksellers or by contacting:

iUniverse LLC
1663 Liberty Drive
Bloomington, IN 47403
www.iuniverse.com
1-800-Authors (1-800-288-4677)

ISBN: 978-1-4917-3908-2 (sc)
ISBN: 978-1-4917-3909-9 (e)

Printed in the United States of America.

iUniverse rev. date: 06/24/2014

With Gratefulness
To Marysia Maziarz Dickson
Author of Polish-American fiction,
who is my delight and inspiration,
and to her children Debbie, Tami and William
—the author

I wish to thank
Nina Barton Owens & Anuška Smith
for sponsoring the celebrated Croatian artist Ella Fleš
to paint the Author's portrait from a photograph by
Einar Berg (black & white rendition on p. viii).

I also wish to thank Einar Berg
for the cover design and dedicated technical support
during the final preparations
of this manuscript.

Think where man's glory must begin and end,
and say, my glory was, I had such friends.
—couplet by Yeats

What Poetry Means To Me

I think poetry is more than an entrance, signification and revelatory ending; or one must be a social historian or human behaviorist to write it, but covers a vast and intimate territory —much closer to the heart.

Poetry carries a metaphoric visa of the imagination allowing the poet to cross creative frontiers of the mind.

Painting: Ella Fleš after photo by Einar Berg

The poet Billy Collins observed that all babies are born with a knowledge of poetry because the rub-dub of a mother's heartbeat is in iambic meter. Then, he said, life slowly starts to choke the poetry out of us. I'm deeply grateful that this year (2014) my poetry archives were requested by and established with the Robert E. Kennedy Library on the Cal Poly campus, San Luis Obispo, California.

—RCD

Contents

BOOK I

Selected Poems

*Most of these poems were previously
published in the following volumes:
Chapbooks,
Parlando (KC Press),
The Press corps of Xanadu (iUniverse),
Wingbeats After Dark (Red Hen Press),
With the Blood of Butterflies (Infinity Pub.).
They were selected by popular request from
over a hundred California readings.*

—the Author

THANK YOU VERY MUCH FOR THE LAST TIME

—Finns do not thank each
other for a visit, but wait
for the next meeting.

Summer days without darkness; winter without light
but for the flare of her body
in firelight; raw/pine rooms, flax/covered chairs,
life brought back
to the 100/year/old bed.
Nakedness steaming in the log/fueled sauna; bodies
color of pink/fleshed salmon trout
found in Baltic inlets; her smell of birch leaves &
juniper berries; her aura, sisu,
a pack with pride & the past.
Toasting with frosted glasses of *kokenkorvo,*
a strong schnapps
biting the teeth of laughter with toasts of *Hei &*
Terveydeksi.

to your health

sharing broiled crayfish in dill with barley bread . . .

He felt, in dying; how that Cheater War
chose young salmon trout,
caught, sealed, gutted; smoked in the dull drone
of gunfire
fed with birch branches & bark shavings
in the round old oildrum of the world,
lost in deep pillows
of arctic cloudberries,
the hot & whirling whiteness of her arm . . .

2

THE KEATSIAN STING

What is this snicking in the bottle,
sulfurous steam-jets in the blood?

Revisiting of a great, great-grandfather
from a Keatsian land of old-bog

Roadhouses, the philanthropy
of long, liquid Scottish lines,

Poetry on the walls? Did he know
the Muse was my visa, voyaging on

Waters of the imagination, sailing,
tipping, sliding, out where rum

Is hard to keep inside the glass
of a world that breaks into a thousand

Crystal fragments before your eyes?

LEGENDS OF TERROR: THE CONCLUSIONS

—Shekh, ancient spelling.

They appear to be listening—
Human ears, dispassionately severed—
An 18th Century Warlord's trophies, color of blood
On heated dirt, fished from barrels of brine
Balanced on the backs of dromedaries,
Strung on walls by the Shekh's faithful, a warning
That an absolute power herein resides; a place
Where a daughter's dowry was rich in ransom notes;
A time when the culture of terror flourished,
Hajji, Muslim pilgrims. Andalusian Moors,
Sacrificed on way to shrines, bodily smell of
Burning flesh, pelatons of swords scissoring
The sun; Time now, to bury the Taliban in graves
Of yellow star thistle, a vicious vacuity closed
At last, as the world awaits the promises of Peace,
And the children listen.

ONLY THE FLIES ARE DIFFERENT

—for Céslaw Milosz

What kind of insanity is this
that tricks the brain
into thinking straight when the world
is steaming like a samovar
of vodka and cucumbers? When must
a young poet
escape the slavery of form, forsake bland
lines
for a driving beat, become something
much more
than futurist or symbolist?
When the search ends in the aura
of place
is it not the poet's duty to find
a national equivalence
for the expression, "Nonsense, my good
man, one must live and that's that.
Shit is always the same everywhere, only
the flies are different."

THE SAINT OF SEMPER FI

—Boot Camp, Marine Corps,1942

Our old Gunny Sgt.'s deployment ribbon
soon became a rainbow stream of stars
we boots vowed to emulate

For country, corps, and the folks back home.
Gunny's voice rose in thunderous power
of pure discipline, unraveling,

At reveille, the sheets on our beds, we said,
in awe of his presence of command,
we raw kids from New York, Chicago,

North Philly and Bend, Oregon, surprised
to find out how old he was, our invite
to his retirement party at a near-by

Off-base slop-shoot near Parris Island,
where Gunny greeted us with a
soft, grand-fatherly voice, rubbed

Our shaved heads; You go where they send
you, lads, with pride in Corps and Country.
Once I had Embassy Duty, stood guard

Out front in hot, shit-speckled sand, town kids
shouting, jeering, trained by the
intefadeh uprising, pelting me with filth,

But I stared strait head as if they were not there,
locked my legs for the long duty like
Ol' Ben, my horse back home
Who could sleep standing up, waiting to
whinny a first greeting for me every
morning, yes boys, bonded,

6

Like we are here together, So I'm retired,
but my back is your back, lads,
wherever you go, I go, because now

You are my children.

CASTANETS

Shell casings sound like castanets
washing in the surf; muted
by the music of flesh, brushed
by wings of carnivorous birds.

What pay-grade earns beauty with death,
as his wife, waiting for mail, hums
to herself, as she hangs out
the morning laundry?

—Author's note:
I was an F.D.O., Fighter Direction Officer,
a captain in the Second Marine Air Wing,
war two, South Pacific Theatre.

SHELL SONG

I listen! Here it comes again!
The susurant, shivering sigh

Of shells I remember as a boy,
Punking a saw on the graveyard shift

In a little eastern Oregon sawmill town,
Sibilant screams of sharpened blades

Slicing tendons of Ponderosa pine,
Slowing down to the mournful whine

Of blades through pitch-knot, the way
We clutch, chew foxhole dirt, scream

For mothers, knowing our tickets
Are punched for the late-night show,

A theatre of the absurd where medics
Are ushers, all tremble in the re-runs

We've seen a dozen times, memorized
Forever on the linings of our hearts.

UNDER THE PANOCOCO TREE

—to M.M.

I choose to write
Under the panococo, a necklace tree
Whose delicacy of light

Transforms the texture
Of thought, once coarsened by wounds
Of the world

To a filature of silk-soft leaves
Tantalizing winds,
As if it knows the precise moment

You will appear, and my pen
Will wing again.

WHISPERS OF THE EVENING TIDE

—for Marysia M.

Day darkening into dusk—
The sea's raw restlessness
stills to a murmurous sigh,
We lie side by side
listening to water
Slip like a silk dress
from the hull, cleave
To the inner flesh
of our breath,
Floating on whispers
of evening tide.

ON THE ESPLANADE

I listen to the click
of wooden needles
as fishermen mend nets
in the white paste fields
of pigeons,
their women waiting and watching
from sea-warped cars
dented like the ocean
in metallic grays and blues.
As a hobo poet
assigned to the underground
each needle click is a spike
tapped on a railroad track
stretching across vast waters.
I owe Borges, the fabulist, nothing.
I read everything and forget
everything
in the customary nick of time.

THE BIRD WOMAN DRESSED IN FRIGATE
BIRD FEATHERS

She lived on the island
Across from the sponge warehouse
In a Danish colonial cottage; kind to strangers,
As if each wounded face was
Christ himself.
He looked like a manatee with propeller scars
From mouth to chin, walked in dripping
Wet from white-fanged suppurations
Of the storm.
She's retired from a folk-dance company
That toured the world,
Tamed wild iguana, West Indian whistling ducks,
Dressed airily in frigate bird feathers
Trimmed with a peregrine falcon's ruff, scent of
Spice islands on her skin; they danced
Together to an old Bob Marley record, her macaw
Sang parodies from an open cage & if,
Perchance, you pay a visit, they'll still be dancing,
Dreamily, more than welcome to whatever
Time & life will bring.

THE LAST WHALE

—to Deborah T.

futtock shrouds of the topmast high seas
gray with distant flensing of bloodied bull whales,
aboard a half-brig, 372 gross ton, 183 foot two-decked
framed with white oak, chestnut planked with long leaf
pine
copper fastened and lost at sea in . . .

a twenty-two year-old kid who wanted to be . . . today
he would be a buff ecologist signed on as assistant
navigator,
young tar-scented gutsy lads, roaring sunburned
sons-of-bitches
posing as words on Conrad's cold & boiling sea, yet
willing

in his soundless calm to breach the roaring forties
of the south latitudes
cosecant to polar distance to
cosine of the half sun

a barnswallow rests on the lazyjack,
310 miles S by E of Bermuda, a porpoise impaled
on a harpoon over the martingale stays
the girls back home like garupas in the water
legs spread for deep diving in the galley
of black-eyed skipjack blue-eyed
albacore dark-eyed blue-lined runner

waiting for a harpooned whale snuffed
to the loggerhead as neatly as an account exec
on the big street of dreams and
what's the difference in a wooden-hulled existence
without care for sea or storm

time to flex his wetsuit, grease lance,
mount the director's larboard boat
pull heavy oars of the board meeting

meeting to order sang the secretarial cooper's order
turning the stone on razor-whetted boarding knives,
wood to the blackskin! blows!

dead ahead! forty-barrel bull abound
this crucifying sea stoked with the hard bread,
water of Club 21

gray overcast strong winds chop the long
swells of cigar smoke as he waits anxiously
for a snick of sun
through lowering clouds of cologne
Miami tans varnished with bull spermaceti
beyond flickering cabin light of whale oil
burning lamps, to sea again
pulling the heavy share, watching a squadron
of bikinied squid bearing contractual documents, blowing
a drowsy sepia-inked screen
before the maggotswarm of sharks
gunning for his ambergris
carefully hidden in his secret belly
in the darkest part of him
but for the buglight lit . . .

the shouted song *Whiskey Johnny*
sung by the ring of bulls
as the larboard boat pounded, fell, rose
in the watch for weather

he adjusted his monkey belt and held the needle
overhead so they could see the color
of his pride in the morning rain

as the foresail goose-winged abanging
high on the swinging mast again

look sharp! raise a whale!
razor-whetted iron at half-cock for Johnson
far at the end of the table, forty-barrel
Johnson who opposed the merger, Johnson,
surfacing and blowing a vaporous nasal spray
of shredded invectives, swimming easily,
smoothly with speed, flukes barely
under the surface

in minutes the kill over the kill over
get over the kill so Johnson's widow
can play with his scrimshaw sperm whale teeth
incised lampblack designs, time

for his widow to bake a lonely pie
crimpin' the gunnel of freshly rolled piecrust
with Johnson's ivory jaggin' wheel, so now . . .

reach in the water and touch Johnson's crinkled
rubbery skin, touch the knobs, partitions,
to see what corporate life is like the instant
before death,

surfacing big bull he is O my God yes he breaks
water back from blowhole to hump
grease the lance take steady aim FIRE!

waifs and wigwags to the skipper

I've got Johnson!

toss out the barrel drogue let him swim
with the line in his bloodstained sea, *harpooned,*

waiting for the bloody boarding knives
to cleave his scarf of blubber, oil tried-out
and casked for home.

MR. TESTUDO, TASTE OF THE HOOK

Mr. Testudo, round and hard
as a turtle shell
had smallpox scars
like hard-driven copper rivets,
veins like bands of red crystals throbbing
in his wrists, strong blunt fingers
flashing an overly-sharpened knife;
a shirtless man, suspenders of mottled eel-skin
snapping over muscles
as he filleted a yellowtail
before a gallery of river rats; contagious grin
infecting all who came to watch
as he performed
with a baton of visceral paradiddles,
the big fish disappearing, gill and tail, silvery
arc of sun, snip of head
erasing taste of hook, released, in mid air,
as if Mr. Testudo had become
a necromancer of salmon spirit, could re-assemble
all it splendor
and make it swim again.

ODE TO A ROPE'S END KNOT

Under a showering of stars
I sail alone at night,
tie a bowline to my waist,
fallen overboard once
for you, this time a sturdy
timber hitch,
a sheepshark, double
blackwall,
cinch a parbuckle down tight,
swinging in a can hook
sling & at last, a rope's end knot,
strong as seasalt, so no way,
on fair or turbulent seas,
you can slip away
again.

ON SURPRISING THE SEA
WASHING HERSELF
IN THE MORNING

The sea washes herself
in a pale pewter bowl.
neck, arms, belly
of the isthmus,
down long peninsula legs,
seaweed tangle,
all over,
behind her veil of spray
until the sun
spills yellowing yolk
on combers,
a tern scatters entrails
of a herring, mouth of channel opens
like a soft silk curtain
as she waves farewell to fishermen
who have been, like me,
watching her, most
avidly.

RED DRUM

There's a full moon over Scorpio's tail
as the old shirtless man with the bony body
sporting scars from the shrimp wars
sits on his empty lot where the tornado
picked the wooden teeth of pilings
clean as a gator's grin.

He sits cooking something the Cajuns
called Red Drum, a pepper-coated, flash-singed,
blackened redfish on a flat tin
supported by two bricks that once connected
a porch to his fishing shanty. He feeds the fire
with splinters from his boat, toasts

The tornado gods with a wicked grin, mocking
tone with touch of awe
without hint of rejection or redemption,
as if every life is swept clean as long white
beaches with mounds like sacks of spilled sugar
curved to fit a woman's body. A natural place
where one can begin again.

THE SIEVERS OF TIME

Grandfather told me about the Chinese
placer miners on the Washington side
of the Columbia River, kneeling, sieving
gold in long windrows of rock plaited
like a mother's hair. The Irishman, O'Halloran
would sing to them in his whiskey tenor,
in full, O wirra, the Irish Muire O Mary,
a sorrowful lament to which they listened
in respectful silence, dreaming of railroad
ties in Chinese porcelain, the river filmed
through a salmon's eyes, beating tails upon
the weir as if thumping the cruelty of time.

SOUTH BAY JESSE

Jesse rode an
Indian 4-cyl Kickstart
like a transition verb
in an old *Indiana Jones* saga;
docked his ketch in the tightest slip
without an engine, trolled
hootchies for halibut in South Bay,
enthralled children tracing color spots
on leopard sharks,
told them bass don't always spawn
in shallow water. got his 10-fish
limit before noon, sped
To the Delta, told stories on the *Sugar Barge*
We still remember.

ON A SWELL OF FEATHER

—for Marysia M.

In the sea's
smoke fog, sky swirling
a Chinese blue,
we listen to the liquescent
outlaws of rhythm,
deep bass boom of combers,
ruffle of the surf snare,
heavy beat of cormorant wing
topping waves
as we sail beside them,
our boat lifting
like love released
on a swell of feathers
into the air.

WINGBEATS AFTER DARK

I have been acquainted
with the night.
—Robert Frost

The moon swings
on a bluesy guitar hook
plucking heartstrings in the sky.
I'm dancing
in a Theodore Rilke poem
with a woman described as lovely
in her bones.
I ask her
will she go with me
where Yeats wrote The Wilde Swans of Coole?
Yes, she says, I want to see
the tincturing of darkness
fall over their whiteness,
hear wing beats of poetry, hush
of oiled feathers
gliding over water, understand
this proud bird, both arrogant and free.

THE PHEROMONES OF THEBES

What is this? Faces rouged by road rage, the heresy
of hearsay, an Orwellian rebellion wired to wooden tongues?

Brains bored to the score, taught to taste the sweet milk
of metaphor? A trash boat powered by nubile neurotoxins,

Songbirds singing the soliloquy of self, a time when women
call a bio-ethicist before the pediatrician, med students

Switching to dinosaur physiognomy, tangled in sea-wrack
wreckage of our senses, startled at life's expectations?

Is all a prickly pain in the panache, satraps of social sadness,
somber suckle of puissant passions, up early with the news teams,

Snout sensitive as cadaver dogs following Copernicus, Kepler &
Galileo dressed in laurel leaf & jungle print checking in to

A tourist's hotel? Write the *Pheromones Of Thebes* within
the scramble of our ids, perfume of poetry flavoring the winds?

THE POLITICAL SAWYERS

The reek
Of red sawmill boards.

The whine
Of saws slowing through pitchknot.

Length, width & breadth of America
Graded, stacked, ready for shipment

On a distant cold November.

A FITTING JUST FOR YOU BY THE TAYLOR
OF TIME

Sometimes life is like a cigar factory reader
reciting Shakespeare, words unfolding in the long aromatic
leaf, floating on waves of sound that could be Jimi
Hendrix's Purple Haze.

Sometimes life is composed of first-hand experience
like a 90-year-old musician of pre-Castro Cuba;
sweating twelve-hour days in a sugar mill, rum's dark
tickling of the testes until you think you're Orestes

In Rio. Sometimes life turns chimeric, everything wildly
fanciful, imaginary, unreal; stoic as a chimera, fire-
breathing monster with lion's head, goat's belly, a
serpent's tail swinging from a swallow-tail tux, a fitting

Just for you by the tailor of time, and when you complain
it isn't you he assures it's merely mythological, and
besides, it's the best, under the circumstances
that he could do.

GRANDFATHER ON VOLTAIRE

I remember grandfather calling me to his room
with the faint scent of Oregon cedar; words

Slowing down like a dry creek to the Deschutes River
outside his window. Gramps was a kind man who

Could leverage love out of the ornery; read a lot—
poets Longfellow, Pope, Gray, scattering

Of the *Federalist Papers* with *Cap'n Billy's Whizbang,*
forgot the meditative melancholy of the body

With the bible and the sports page—
'One life can change another,' he said, 'Live yours

For others—hope—peace—be a leader—
think of a quarterback who moves out of life's

Tight pockets, throws accurately, moves the chains—
don't face social doldrums like Sirius, The Dog Star,

Barking at the moon—
down to a hoarse slow trickle of sound. Remember

Voltaire, son, the end of *Candide,* "Let your garden grow."'

UPON THE 20th ANNIVERSARY OF
CONDUCTOR MICHAEL NOWAK
WITH THE SAN LUIS OBISPO SYMPHONY

And as I wake, sweet music breathe,
Above, below, underneath,
Sent by some spirit to mortals good,
Or th' unseen Genius of the wood.
L 'Allegro,
   —John Milton, 1608-1674

We begin with praise—
A bravura *allegro con brio,* the opening—
For there are no endings to music,
The art of sound and time,
Sculpted in Michael Nowak's name; his signature
On *every* note, textured, spinning the gossamer touch
Of air—
Arpeggios soaring, whispers of *pizzicato,*
Sound of flowers in the woodwinds
Perfumes the ethos of his care.
We are enraptured by Michael's introductions,
Significance of worldly compositions
Spoken in dry and antic wit
A musicologist from Juilliard would gladly share.
A consummate musician, master
Of the viola's joys and throbbing sorrows,
Enhancing films, recordings,
Chamber music laurels adding luster
To his score.
May our maestro continue his own *libretti,*
Godspeed, *accelerando,* ennobling
The Symphony's traditions
For another twenty years, or more.

THREATENED SPECIES

—to Pat P.

Gramps looks like a red-legged frog
    in his board shorts, a prime
Example of the Threatened Species Act
    on his new paddleboard
Winding through kayaks and big boarders,
    skimming like an osprey over
Quiet water, eight-ft. board and wetsuit
    honorably retired; with boyish
Grin waves at the birder convention
    on shore, not knowing
They are watching a rare ivory gull,
    not taking a picture of him.

THE FERRARI LOVE SONG

—to Rich W.

Unrequited love, says Pancha Psychela,
my emotional mechanic,
is like driving your Ferrari around town
at 20 m.p.h.—
you should take that sucker to Arizona
or Wyoming, blow it out at 150,
limber up its formidable juices, paste your
windshield with bugs of the season,
put a case of Guinness in the boot,
flat-out open the gate to the escape of valves,
cylinders leap-frogging
over the red-lined tach for a taste of speed,
scream out into the wind
until your face is Ferrari red, blow kisses
from your driver's gloves
perforated for pit-stop passions, and after
you have garaged the beast
remember your co-piloto, carelessness
of throttle, spinning out
into the chicane of loss, together.

THE RUNNER

What I want to do is run to the limits of
consciousness.
—Steve Prefontaine, Hayward Field,
University Of Oregon, Eugene

Only the white lime lanes of Hayward Field
could hold him on this earth; legs churning, drawn
into the vortex of the centrum, air burning acetylene fires
in the lungs, arms high, close to ribcage as if to hold
a swarming scream of birds; scissoring through
Oregon's rain-rinsed air blue with fog, out in front,
flat out, right leg crossing left as fresh waves
of crowd-roar follow him in the turns; the pack behind,
pushing him on, soft thud of spiked shoes on packed
cinders, tight burn down back of legs, without ease
of drafting, heart on the clock locked in a box
where speed has thrown away the key; a choreographer
instructing oxygen how to dance with flesh, curtain
closing on the musculature of madness, pain searching
for answers, selfless, a secret language he must learn
in the swift blur of sports semantics, dialogue with
the gods who wait at the finish line with a foil-slash
of tape across his chest, unlock the gates, let him in
before the last hushed rush disappears behind his eyelids,
lost in faraway explosions, a winner refusing to be left
uncrowned, unsung.

—Author's note: *I received a track and field scholarship at the*
University of Oregon, Eugene; '39- '42. My coach, 'Colonel'
Bill Hayward, was national Olympic coach until games were
cancelled by World War II. I served in the U.S. Marine Corps
as a captain, South Pacific theatre. The '08' Olympic Trials
were held at Hayward Field, the same track I ran on 66 years
earlier.

HONEY IN YOUR MIND

I admired the Coptic monk
who didn't proselytize

As he sat beside me
on the bus to Cadiz.

'You pray and pray until
you get it right,' he said,

'Pray and pray until your prayer
becomes honey of the mind,

And the taste of your soul is good.'

THE DESKTOP DIALOGUES

He who seeks rest, finds boredom.
He who seeks work, finds rest.
—Dylan Thomas, Welsh author
and poet, 1904-1953

As sure as Ananias was struck dead for lying,
truth separates the social psyche:

The op-ed page, once the rage, has now gone
Blogovian   3-D games, titular topic, leave
our kids myopic   Grandmother tweets as she
sweeps   Desktops pop at bus-stops   All seem
gorged on megabytes of mirth   Get your smarts
in liberal arts   Four beats a link, Jazz, Indie,
Country, Pink   Pop-Culture's bio-boomers take
in roomers   If erotic becomes toxic, mannequins
will shake their coccyx   Get your belly full,
right on time, of filibuster's bitter brine   Take note
when deciphering, WikiLeaks needs diapering
If windshield dolls don't enthrall, let them shimmy
up the wall   When history unfolds its wings, a
buzzard sings   Unbutton the button-downs, bring on
the clowns   Homegrown terror plots are thick,
nightsticks won't do the trick   Beware brokering
of nuclear death, its silky whispering of stealth
We must not cower at plenary power, story of Whig
and Tory   Thought sought, bartered, traded, flag of
the heart, un-faded   Water boy sits by a drying
spring, no song of hope to sing   Polar bears carry
signs of warning, scrawny cubs of global warming
War is grief catatonic, blood and tears un-economic.

Words form, dissolve, imperishable with meaning:

Righteous or perditious, climate change of man's
Condition   Theocrites had poems compelling,
true to love in all its telling   Equality's gap agape,
rich and poor escalate   All tantric intonations

30

echo from despairing nations   Is compassion out
of fashion, morphed to illusions, mystical and
profound, or is this where sweet love is found?
A little politesse, no more, no less   Carbon
footprints in the sand, lead to a selfish contraband,
Pat-downs in stations of our fears,
Arrears of jobless in the middle   Who
work hard, sweat out the riddle,   Does
mournful melancholy contain laughter
of our folly?   Siesta of the soul   Play
the Super Bowl?   Tribes of vibes
turn docents of decency?   Energy an
anomaly?   Antic, frantic? Pilotos sotto?
Software sources driving Porches, waving
back to weeping women, a style in exile, not
forgiven?   Should we monetize a world unwise,
try to please, find a job overseas?   Survive
a laconic economic,   Time the real power,
strong enough to crush the hour?   That's
what I've plenty of,   Ask the mourning
dove, sitting on my windowsill   Despite chill,
grey as fossil fuels burned by fools,   I have no
dossier, words to say,   Have you ever lived on
poet's pay?   Brushed by breath on glass,
alas, I'm no Donne, Herrick, Shakespeare mimic,
Con a clinic   Take a gong   For my ragged song,
from the world of Da Da?   Or even pity from my
mentor, Octavio Paz, Mexico City?   Some say
poems are written   To be given away   A swift relay,
So dear mourning dove, I script on glass   This tome
at last   May it live long as Poe's 'The Raven'
Let's vex the text   Pretend it's a real depression,
Life's lesson   Wear raiments of reality   Unfolds
for young and old—

Too alliterative, wing-brush of the mourning dove,
as if to explain not all's insane, its eyes
are digital dots, fiery spots, yet wistful in the traffic
drone as the city empties, and we're alone.

OL' CAP NEVO

Back when rip-rap was not the high jive
of youth, but secured weak Delta walls,
my friend told me the the story of 'Ol
Cap Nevo who drove to the dock
in a $50 levee car, a junker he'd drive
until the wheels came off at the junkyard
door, a sad preview yet to come:

One day Ol' Caps's work boat with
a ballast of cement mixers left Angel
Island for Tiburon. skipper would
hold cap over heart as they passed that
grim rock pile called Alcatraz, a depository
of misdeeds, when suddenly, hull ripped
out on submerged pylon—

My friend saw pain on the old man's face
in light of the flare gun as they pulled
him from the cuddy, although mortally wounded
he would chide them on what death meant to
him: Listen kids, we're all going to take a ride
someday in that big black limo, remember
the old western, forgot who wrote it—

> *Spend your money but don't look back,*
> *You'll never see a hearse with*
> *A luggage rack ....*

The harbor boat saved all but him, and when
the crew thawed out that night, my friend said
they toasted Ol' Cap Nemo, each too young to
joke about lives they hadn't lived, but would
borrow a little of his courage, set courses,
one by one, with variations deep within.

WHY THE LIVING ARE HARD-WIRED TO THE DEAD

Is it a teleprompter
Who speaks for the supplicants
Of shame, retrofits rhythms
Of our greed, throws boots at
The bad-asses, cancels out
The corruptible, shoulders blame?

Who rocks the cradle
Of the acculturated, yearns for grace
Before bread, or a minister at
A funeral, explaining why
The living spirit
Is hard-wired to the dead?

WHEN THE RAINS CAME

When the rains came
The older couple sat holding hands
In the backseat of a military sedan; wipers
Clicked slowly through a surge
Of sudden water drumming on the roof like
Far-off artillery—

The volunteer driver with gentle voice
Parks in a blur of white markers
Disappearing in misted tendrils,
Turns, touches gloved hand with theirs,
"I know how you feel." he says,
"My son rests here with yours."

"I like the rain," the mother says,
"Let's stay here a while longer,
perhaps the rain will wash
all the wars away—"

33

CAMOFLEUR

Before I write another word, signatured
The sights and sounds of a wounded world,

Not as a camofleur who can cleverly disguise
The agonies within us, let me choose to follow

> *My friends transposed to the jobless,*
> *Vets as bo's chased by yard bulls,*
> *Cracked skulls with hickory clubs,*
> *Listened, with them, to the coal hopper's*
> *Metallic rattle, a reefer car's sighs and*
> *Moans, no place along the line to shave*
> *And shower, press a suit for an interview,*
> *Back to sunsets bandaged in reddish mauve,*
> *Seep of unstitched sorrows, the same two-*
> *Lane asphalt that runs beside us, as if*
> *Seeking solace of the train, an integer of*
> *Other wars our grandfathers fought*
> *Fiercely in sun and rain; this long road,*
> *Once a rustic rut, a stubborn track for*
> *1928 Model A's . . . .*

We've developed an enormous hunger for all forms
Of decency, stand, salute from the siding
The Midnight Limited with glowing candelabra
In the dining car, a porter's silhouette as he pulls
Down sheets in the Pullman: Then, the fleeting
Glaze of light has gone, we wonder if the passengers
Of peace had disappeared, and in the sky,
How far the star?

THE GARIMPEIRO: A TRANSLATION

*. . . The prospector along the Rio Madeira River rushing
below the Brazilian shield called the long cemetery . . .*

Sun, a suturing surgeon splitting a thousand s's—
stench/stuporous/servitude/a thousand *gurimpos*—
(prospectors, *Señor*)
a thousand sons-of-bitches housed in dark jungles
roofed in green
listening to atabrine-yellow parrots
squawking *bamburrado!*
(we struck it rich, *Señor!*)
Radio's relief. Snooded against the sun snake. Daily fix
of London gold, all watched over by *Curio*
(beautiful black bird of destiny, *Señor*)
amused by theft, murder, claim-jumping,
sitting in skittish light
branching to sweetsmelling darkness, tumescent overseer
of domed scandals
not unlike the city's cycle of birth, dying, decay . . .
a whore flown in with an aircompressor,
she sweats, works hard as the *garimpeiro* on his rafts,
gravel pumps—
someone to quiet earth movers in the brain.
A world of flaming *formigas*
(we are like ants, *Señor*)
gurimpos wearing greenstone belts of volcanic rock,
washing gold from navels, always scouring,
scourging, searching for *fococo*
(fresh gold, *Señor*)
like a French pig taught to sniff and snout out the truffle—
deep in the swamppit after *fococo*, in the dark hole
where corpses remain to the end of shift,
taming the smoking cobra filling the sluice box,
brains seeping earth, mined pits washing the *Serra Peloda*,
babbling *lost gold, lost gold* . . .
Curio knows. She knows where it all goes, *Señor*.
Perhaps to a banker-or a bum on the bowery of your New York
City. Poof! Lost gold. Plucked

from empty wire crowning stumps on an old alcoholic's teeth—
but, what the hell, that's life, *Señor*
would you like to own one percent
of a good *barranca?*

Señor?

—*Originally published in The Beloit Poetry journal*

A NIGHT WITH THE ZONIANS

I hear the *brujas* as brawling with the *maleantes*
in my room over the expatriates' bar in Colon, aptly
named for the asshole collection of the world:
Columbian supply boats snuffing like swine
among tankers & freighters strung like dark steel beads
on the throat of hell

Electric wires outside my window dance nakedly, spitting
yellow/green sparklers on sugar cane workers with rain-
squall eyes

Looking up at the three-story mural of Bob Marley
in streaks of rainbow color, dreds writhing down bullet-
pocked plaster like jungle pythons

I'm tossing off nightmares like straight shots
of *aguardiente,* head throbbing on hard hotel pillow,
half-listening to the city's slippery slop
of an all-night laundry

Washing cycles of drug money in the bar below—sailors,

bosn's—a gravedigger showing tip of a royal tibia
from an oilcloth package; a place where evening newsprint
goes to bed woozy & wavering, drunk with political power

Waft from whores sprinkled with expensive Paris perfume
in lieu of showers, smell of hot tar cooling, reviving
boyhood of Oregon's blue highways back of Bend
to Prineville, sniffing grandpa's red can of gasoline
for his tractor, the smell of Galveston & oilfields
exploding in my senses

The dream dissolving, reappearing, gigantic painted heads
with tiny dervish bodies parading in Rio, flesh twitching
on the beat, visceral voodoo of the drums

Fumbling for my passport, the bottle, gathering nerve
for the nightly meeting I arrange for my blessing:
the black Madonna of Czestochowa who comes all the way
from Poland, stops to bless my friend Hank B. before
flying through my window in early morning hours

To meet the Black Christ of Portobelo I found halfway
between Colon & San Blas who knocks softly on the door;—
they do nothing but hold hands at the foot of my bed,
whispering to each other, deciding where I must go
from here, what I must do, where we'll rendezvous again

Will it be a series of one-room sanctuaries or a house
with white fence, sound of babies & female laughter,
or how to erase the ugly stigmata on my forehead from the
porcelain bowl that is my shrine & in stop praying there
will it ever fade away?

LA ROSE DE CHEVREFUILLE

when the lithesome sound called Jass
slips off her silk kimono
embroidered with blue peacocks
flying over water, Mistress Jass strolls naked
on the *Vieux Carre* in search of him,
the old New Orleans musician with white
peppercorn hair snugged tight
as a lambswool cap, chin on the lionheaded curve
of cane, touching fiery rim of embouchure,
an intaglio like Satchmo's
fired in the forge of 5000 one-night stands,
circle of pinkish-red on bluish-black, his calling
card with a tiny tit at the top, trace metals
from the hornbite, curious coda stirring
afterflesh of Storyville, oasis of the sporting life,
shivery sounds of the Professor's open-back piano
with madame's beads strung over wire, seated
like a dreaming Buddha before his box
etched in white ginburns on dark mahogany,
long blue smolderings of cigarettes like furry
caterpillars dozing in the weep of wood; to touch,
converse with Mistress Jass
when warm night wind from the Pontchartrain
riffs water like a deck of cards, feel her arms
reaching out to him, skin shimmering under steamer lights
of red & green, beguiling figure like his horn
coaxing salivated runs from breast to belly,
up & down the scale of scented flesh
without a breath
but for the pounding exhalation when abandoned
on the beach of love, the pudenda's pink wave
peels back like a conch shell
meeting morning tide; lovestruck fool, he & his mistress
twisted in sheets of cheap hotels, sleeping,
eating in busses, cars, all saved by the stiffening spine

called the blues, a survival training
like a big lavender bruise found in blood of copper,
umber, in chicory & bourbon, in grinning white & black
piano keys
with stains of nicotine; father's legs propped up
on an apple box, cardboard soles of his shoes,
the old man pointing his bottle at the human swarm
below their window
like a Caesar observing the Tiber . . .
yes, he could tell Jass things few mortal ears
could comprehend
like the time shared that September in Paris,1939
when Germany declared war on Poland; sipping *aperitifs*
at lunch with fellow musicians in the *Chez Berthe*
where Django Reinhardt in pajamas & slippers lunched
with black American musicians
across the street from the Hot Club on *Rue Chantol*
(always a few icons he carried cases for as a boy)
absorbing the anxious moment
when the word was out: the Nazis have declared Jazz
verboten, no after-beat, no *jazzflukens* . . .
remember, little Jass, the damnfool National Socialists
gave edicts to the *Kulturkommen*
so Benny Carter & Coleman Hawkins, fresh from Amsterdam
said, let's cancel all our gigs, get the hell out of
this tin-ear country before we all make chimney music;
Louis Armstrong & Earl Hines received the warning, turned
back home. Jimmie Lunceford cancelled his tour of France,
while you & I, little one, stayed on—
met Django & his brother playing gypsy guitar songs
like "Nuages" & "Manoir de mes Reves"
for bouillabaisse & beer in the horsemeat butcher shop
& used-shoe store (a Django Reinhardt record on black
market was worth two kilos of butter, then . . .)
"Les Petits Swing" or "Zazous" (after Cab Calloway's
Zazouzazous scat singing) lazed in Dadaistic virtues
of the Zazou Cafe, wore pegged pants, baggy knees,
high-rolled English collars; kitsch to wear

Hitler mustaches, sport yellow stars if you weren't
Jewish, carry a Chamberlain umbrella.
the French were good to us, slyly booked in *La Garrone,*
Chez Florence (where the maitre'd knew all the snobs),
La Cabone Cabaine where we played for the first
customer to arrive & the last to leave, & for a glass
of pernod
I'd triple-tongue above high-C, get down in lower register
with gutter roll of lip & tongue.
Remember—we'd jam after hours with Big Bob Goody
at the *Music Box*
with mutes & windows locked & when the band broke up
at dawn we'd catch a charcoal-burning taxi, fear of Nazis
thick as its blue exhaust
weaving through their big 500 K staff cars, Panhards
& Citroens, headlights painted blackout blue
sweeping away terrified pigeons
with horned feet scritching cobblestones . . .
Only moneyed Nazis bought champagne, celebrating
the invasion of Poland, sat up front
at the little bandstand at the *Chez Florence*
listening—
yes, sweet Mistress Jass—I'd bite my mouthpiece & the
bullet when they seated the strutting fools,
knowing time had come to re-title songs in French
(jazz became *verboten)*
tricked their obdurate ears with "The Saint Louis Blues"
announced as "La Tristesse de Saint Louis" a Nazi favorite, played
with icy edged bonhomie; "Ma Chère Susanne"
for "Sweet Sue" & your very favorite—"Honeysuckle Rose"
disguised as "La Rose de Chevrefuille" still holding
memory's scent, captured in the small fresh rosebud
in my buttonhole
as you let your hair down & dance divinely along the levee
once again.

FAILURE IN THE FOLDEROLS

To be an artist is to fail, as no other dares fail.
That failure is his world and to shrink from it
Is desertion, arts and crafts, good-housekeeping . . .
                          —Samuel Beckett

The new poem, muted, listless as a long uncorked wine,
stirs sullenly, a feckless gesture,
kicking my ass out of bed. The woman eating the mango
is making love to her ex-husband.
The water drip is tickling tangos in my feet.
The cardboard cut-out of Christ, face bright with
Madame's nail polish, stands tall, towering
over her dresser
beside the Spanish edition of the Gideon bible.
The tip jar is crying for *pesetas*
below his painted tears.
The poem, so far, appears disquieting, an engine
on enigmatic,
I will ask it to put something on, wait in the park
by the carousel.
I must remember—each poem speaks to itself,
hoping the reader is listening,
that all goes well.

GRAMP'S GRIPE

I don't understand it at all,
said Gramps,
here I am at ninety-two,
a 3-D seismic of my pulse o.k.,
life's taught me a lot, been
good to me, I obey all protocols,
try to be friendly, environmentally,
wear my reusable diapers
when I go to town, still don't know
why I owe those damn student
loans

UNCLE NED AND LITTLE PHOEBE

Uncle Ned, curator of family wit and candor,
towered over his 5-ft.wife, Little Phoebe.
Uncle told us Little Phoebe was socially active,
loved parties, but extremely unable to hold
her liquor. It so happened, said Uncle, one
particular party had become memorial; he'd
felt ebullient himself, swung Little Phoebe
over his shoulder, said goodbye to hosts,
turned for the door, when Little Phoebe gave
a tiny fart *goodnight*.

UNCLE CLARENCE AND
THE ANIMALS ON TV

Uncle Clarence can't suppress what he sees
On TV, calls out to Aunt Nedda in another room,
This time it's an animal show, 'Lookit—
Lions hate the sound of baboons—
Giraffes sleep five minutes a night—
Male hyenas eat their young—and—wait
To you see this—rhinos fart through
Their mouths just like our politicians.'

IN THE DOG PARK OF DREAMS

He adjusted his stylish Mutt Mitt gloves,
brushed off from his dog's mouth
the lathering lick of love—
they would share the new park's excitement—
a social event with other—
perhaps he would see (she wore no rings)
the owner of little FiFi—
his Homer had sniffed so joyously, and yes,
vigorously—
showed off, with pride, his vaccination tag—
here, in this new freedom for beast
& man—out at last
from the dog pound of loneliness—
that is, until the owner of that corrosive Chow
without a leash, the guy who owned
the Maserati, would be horning in again.

THE KID IN THE STEEL-TOED BOOTS

first day on the rig, a hot and dusty day
  in his stiff steel-toed boots
    down in the weevil's corner
    waving up
    to the Tower Monkey
    in his cowboy hat

    under the twin diesel roar
    drill stem jutting up, up—
    down a mile
    sixty feet a spit

over the turntable, rotating the drill stem
  the kid in the steel-toed boots
  seals new pipe, winched to the tower
    the kid winks at the driller
    hunching over his controls
    in the Weevil's Corner

the youthful smile fades
  as he slips in his steel-toed boots
  impaled on the drill stem skewer,

round and around, a crimson pinwheel,
gleaming, steel-tipped in the sun

the Tower Monkey looks hard
  at the kid lying dead in the doghouse shed,
  the kid in the steel-toed boots.

THE KING OF STRIPPER WELL

the old man
  smells of thick, black crude
  sitting on his oil patch throne
  a stripper well in Noble county

     rolling dice most every day
     playing 25-cent limit poker
     win $5 and go home happy

the old man's down, down
  to the bottom of the barrel
  oozing like a great black wound
  bound with the cries of roustabouts

near the end
  he had a dream
  striking natural gas—
  a million cubic foot a day . . .

now, the old man wears
  a pin-stripe suit
  spattered spats, four-in-hand cravat
  wading around in gulf coast leases
  selling other folks' dreams
  a briefcase as his office

     get your barn burner, folks!
     sign your barn-burner with me today
the old man
  parks his pick-up walks at night
  at night the lights look like stars
  on the drilling rigs

he counts the ships of light
  knowing each unlit star is his.

SPRINKLED ON THE SEA

I see her face

    backlit with flowers,

Hair tangled, a wild

    garden, body warm

As cinnamon

    sprinkled on the sea.

REQUIEM FOR O'HALLORAN

I'm ashamed of myself. I sound like a baby seal
snuffling in the dark. I pretend we're on an old
square-rigger, I'm returning to the seaman's Dog
House thinking of my friend O'Halloran's body,
washed, anointed with a splash of Old Bushmill,
sewn in canvas, weighted with ballast rock,
Captain intoning the burial-at-sea prayer,
bell striking 13 as O'Halloran slides down the
carpenter's board to be welcomed by old King Neptune
instead of slumbering in a galley reefer, toe tagged
for the port of Los Angeles, heat slipping down
the long slab hull toasting the interdecked Toyotas.

SO WHEELS CAN KEEP THEIR PROMISES

I've got a feeling like when
you unpack your bag in your old room
back home. I'm in a gondola car
round as Buddha's belly
sitting on a load of river gravel,
a safe steel-ribbed place with great acoustics
so at night I can sing to the stars.
The track inspector walks by, head down
as if dreaming of jackpots in Las Vegas.
I'm waiting for the engineer to play
his instrumental solo on the whistle
so wheels can keep their promises,
become spark-scattering worlds,
whirling, rounding out the miles
until choked to death by the brakeman
at a siding in my hometown.

A pot of fresh flowers marked *Papa*
  reserved his favorite barstool
as he sat with tourists whose drinks
  held festive little umbrellas of
palm. *Theatrum mundi,* he'd laugh,
swirling his fine rum and lime.
Warmed by its taste he told
  of an old village fisherman
who swore that pepper in a boat's
  caulking tar prevented barnacles
as sure as practitioners of *la*
  prostitución ignored pleas of indigent
men; knew winners of the last ten years'
  Sam McGuire trophies in Gaelic football;
hunting in Tanganyika; revealed W.B. Yeats
as a member of a secret society known
as The Order of the Golden Dawn.
  After hours of reciprocal toasting,
he held out his hand that wrote
  The Snows of Kilimanjaro, turned palm
between calluses, pointed to the Rising
  Mound of Apollo, Mound of the Moon, and,
with a playful tap on the bottom of the
  schoolteacher from Iowa, the Girdle of Venus;
aroused his chauffeur, a good-bye to all,
  returned to Mary at the Vinca Vigia,
looked a long time at his tall writing desk
  that stood like a skeleton brooding
for flesh, no swashbuckling sounds but the sea.

MOTHER'S DAY IN MON O'WAR CAY

"You want to buy a big crayfish, mon?"
It was a giant Bahama lobster, eight-
inch head across, foot-long with
at least a four-pound tail. "I'll take
the tail," I said, unbuttoning my shirt
pocket. "And pay for the rest if you'll
give it to your mother." I get senti-
mental about mothers on Mother's Day.
A big woman sat nearby in a scarlet
headscarf & hungry looking eyes.
"I have no mother, mon, but Honoré
shall be my mother today, if you say so.
Honoré must be very hungry, mon,
starving for salvation by the way
she treats her whores."

IN THE BARBADOS

In the Barbados blood mingles; tributaries
of mestee, yellow quadroon; the heart is a sugar
mill pumping sweetness; rum lime punch
from a turtle shell; life is a full crop of cane,
always someone who'll wash a sailor man's
lonely linen for a small coin, a smile for change.

DELTA PEAT

I hear the sound
of a floating clamshell dredge
            licking steel lips
chomping on decayed tules
            heaped on a double-trailer
side-dump truck;
            tons of rich, black
Delta peat
            used on fancy gardens
or in Hollywood war movies,
            its dark glossy pelt
unlike common dirt
            disintegrates in starshells
for the lenses, diabolical
            explosions
luring excitement
            as if rushes were sprinkled
with living blood
            thrilling directors, and, most of all
            the actors, who want to die
dramatically, conveniently,
            without burdensome medals,
row on row of purple hearts,
            oak leaf clusters.

20/20

Sea green as April grass, flourishing
of fishflesh
under the surface; warm wink of the sun's
eye. I can see San Francisco
off the port bow, Coit Tower, the Transamerica
pyramid, sea lions at Pier 39's K-deck,
tourists waiting to board the Red & White Fleet
dock; a woman waving a white hat
as she steps off the No. 30 municipal bus.
She must be waving at me. I wave back
just as a man meets her. They embrace.
I feel the first cold touch of San Francisco
fog, hear the faint hungry cry
of the seals, mocking screech of the gulls.

STARS FALLING OFF INTO THE SEA

There is an uneasiness in paradise
as if soldiers are sleeping on the beaches

Celtic inculcations
stored in vats of Yeats

Dreaming of little islands where taxes
are paid in fruit and fish

Whales sleep with closed eyes like stand-
up bass players at two in the morning

Grief is a sky sequined with feathery clouds
and spirit gum, stars falling off into the sea

POEM FOR STARVING DOE AND FOAL

In light blazed by buck rubs
on low oaks
near the lake ringed by a necklace
of blue ice, the doe stands
shivering
to the foal's rough tongue, last
nuzzling of the teats' torn pinkness,
foal sliding to knees
in shadow of its mother's belly
like a small forest angel
praying to the gods of hunger
in a vaulted apse of snow and stone.

RIDERS OF THE IRON HORSE

Click of tappets
from the old Indian classic
sound like the Sandman
tapdancing around my brain
flying low down two-lane highways
of Washington & Montana,
clockless troubadours, leather saving
our wind-whipped asses, open
air, dust, asphalt, sagebrush,
wildflowers, slowing down
for the Big Horn sheep of Sturgis,
mecca of metal, on to Deadwood,
revving, roaring, awakening
mannequin whores
waving to us from the upstairs window.

PORT ORFORD CEDAR

Our hearts are empty
        as an ocean cove
rinsed of tide; oars stir
        a seep of bearded
seasop in the search
        for the drowned village
daughter, parents, friends
        stand warming
by a beachfire
        listening to the ting
ting ting
        of temple bells
struck by three Shinto priests,
        visitors from Nagoya,
who in the name of grief
        have delayed their mission:
purchase of Port Orford cedar
        for Shinto shrines,
augment their forests
        disappearing into elaborate
sidings, sushi bars, all
        forgotten in the sharing
of these noble trees, the girl's
        coffin, a wood now weeping
in the earth.

—Author's note:

When I read Barry Lopez's *River Notes,* 1975, Ken Kesey's *Sometimes a Great Nation, 1964,* and the books of Anais Nin I am proud and thankful for Oregon authors. I was inspired not only by diaries and memoirs of pioneers, but by my pioneer family itself, coming by wagon train from Independence, Missouri, arriving in the late 1840s settling in the mid-Columbia river country. Here was a swirling cornucopia for the poet's pen: hayers, cooks, mothers, fathers, grandparents, mail carriers, laundresses, loggers, ranchers, cowboys, fishermen, shopkeepers, school teachers, writers, poets. In this humming hive of survivalists and cheerful anarchists there was and is a hardcore love affair for land and neighbor. All seemed to believe Carl Sandberg's, *Nothing can happen if first not a dream.* No Oregon author, historian, or philosopher, could have lived James Joyce's life of 'silence, cunning and exile' as one critic said. It would be hard indeed to separate public vocabulary from the private.

LUMBERCAMP SOUNDS: 1938

—In the Ochoco Forest near Bend, Oregon

Sounds of Cookie's triangle
ting   ting   ting   ting   ting   ting

Splash of cold wellwater in chipped tin basins,
      vinegar flapjacks spitting in wild pig grease,
coffee hot enough to scald. *Click click* of poker
chips on hand-hewn tables, bunkhouse banter,
tobacco shred caught in a mouth-harp's teeth,
sound of a mountain dulcimer played by a
three-fingered man, banjo's twangy thrum. Outside,
black workpants whip like flags of independent
nations, frozen on the barrack's lines.
      Donkey engines like old asthmatic loggers coughing
steam, chains rung with sound of iron bells
      on far ridges, cables flail like snapping snakes,
pok pok of wedges driven in a treefall's moan.

Sounds between curse and prayer: dreaded *swishhhhh*
      of a broken cable thrashing, mowing down legs,
like a McCormack reaper, legs that danced the two-
      step, walked down aisles of country churches;
sucked in breath of choker-setter as fingers fly
      from glove, or the final sound, a sigh

Soft as a wounded bird trapped under crush of log,
Olle Olson, our friend from Stockholm, letters
folded, buttoned in shirt pocket, creased like road-
maps to heaven. Olle breathing bubbles fresh
with blood, last words rising on air's cold currents
returning in axe-quick chips of courage
spilling down the mountainside.

A DAY ON THE DELTA

—to Wolfgang and Beth

The Dutra tug spins a light film of silt
on the San Joaquin River, sky textured,
pale as honeybee wax
over the Stockton turning basin
where deepwater ships stand sleepily
loading, unloading their gorge.
A Japanese deckhand from the *Tokyo Maru*
waves at three Philippinas walking
to Beauty College classes, they wave back,
laughter trilling good-naturedly,
sun warming green skirts of the tules,
a crane, preening, stands on one leg
on a channel marker. The tug captain waves
at me, I salute back from my hatch with
my morning mocha; the Delta groans softly,
earth rich with fragrant promises,
she yawns like a satisfied woman, pushing
day laborers from her bed, permitting
the day to begin, first trickle of sweat
down a backbone
stirring pent-up fury of the sun.

PARADE OF THE BIG SPIRIT SALMON

We sit together
in a little beer bar in The Dalles, Oregon—
the white kid who lies about being a writer
and the old Indian in the John Deere cap
who doesn't have to lie about anything; I
call him Chief. He has intersecting creases,
burned-over trails merging into a sundown color,
obsidian black eyes glittering with Bud,

between deep, undercurrent English
he speaks wet Chinook, cries dry Indian—
knowing high & low water of the roily Columbia,
salmon packed in wet gunny sacks,
times when you could take your fish to town . . .

the Chief points his beer toward the window,
and the Elks float's airhorn hooting & braying—
in the old days they paid you $2.50 a day,
he says,
if you dressed in full regalia,
the Big Spirit Salmon was good to us—
plenty of money—credit was good—The Dalles
was a prime used car market, every brave
had a Buick—
he winked and I bought . . .

the Chief thanks me with a touch of his cap:
in the dim light it becomes a warbonnet
on a long-beaked bird,

slowly we stack ten dead Indians
on the sudsy side
of the long mahogany shore (he talks between
meticulous silences)

when big fall salmon hit the dipnets of a thousand

Treaty Indians, many of whom drowned,
my father and uncle are with the Big Spirit Salmon—

glassy nudge of bottles, the toast, sound
of The Dalles High School marching band,

there is talk of this in the shade of the fish-
house at Tumwater
where we little Indian boys would sit
by big piles of watermelons, bonus for the salmon,

small boys caught salmon heads from the gut box
(shared by all on the reservation),
salmon heads drying in the sun,
I can still see the eyes, flystung, following
me . . .

spurting, darting VFW miniature cars cut across
his words,

our friend, the river, was good to us—
we always gave back part of the best;
from the Government House at Big Eddy
running The Dalles-Celilo canal, head of Five Mile
Rapids,
downstream to Three Mile Reef, from the Seine Bar
to the Oregon Landing,
Fishweil scows on Big Island, Lone Tree Pine Village
to Seafert's China Pete,
to the buying station at Downe's Channel
we followed the Spirit Salmon . . .

we knew the river's bad side,
as every man is good and evil—

did I hear him right?
give back our best to the river?
cold, root-tangled river, washing & writhing,
current, cunning & cruel,

a rock-splitted, white-gutted spilling,
nurturing spirit for the
big salmon dying?

outside in the heat & dust, big splay-footed,
red-nosed clowns
bobbing to curb-bound children,
offering all-day suckers the color of wildflowers,
reds, greens, blues & salmon pink . . .

I tell the Chief I have plenty beer,
if I step outside, why, they'll pick me up
like they did in San Diego—

better now, white son—
he chug-a-lug a half-bottle—

there was a time they wouldn't lock the cell door
on the old jail down by the Union Pacific;
I'd be sleeping off a binge, wake up & walk out—
they'd catch up with me
down by the mail line of the SP & S, charge me
with *breaking jail*—

I hear the Chief's first laugh,
it is taunting & full of life—

suddenly he stops laughing, pushing back
his beer,
encouraging me to see something he sees,
pointing at the wall,
I follow his long, strong, straight-arrow finger—
all I can see is an old, dusty, tacked up
sombrero—

but I hold, steady, then it happens—
I see a giant Big Spirit Salmon
swimming toward us through the wall.

AT THE SAWYERS' JAMBOREE

—Bend, Oregon

I watch two loggers set a saw
for a single buck: wait for the sound
I heard as a boy—

Crisp spits of wood spiraling
in the sun. *Skirrrr Skreeee,*
Skreeee Skirrrr . . . . .

Of the long pull against the clock,
teeth sharp enough to shave
hob-nail beards

Hoping to receive a trophy cup
at the Fourth of July dance
tonight.

THE TOUCH OF TIME

—for Eubie Blake, trumpet, vocal

It's the touch of time, I tell myself,
blurring of gray hair in the mirror.
I search for my collector's disc,
Eubie Blake, the oldest trumpet man around.
I remember one of Eubie's nightly gigs
at a small Manhattan boite, how the drinkers &
the lovers quieted down when Eubie blew
his signature song, cradled horn in arms
like a great-grandchild of Papa Jazz,
sang I Guess I'll Get The Papers And Go Home
for the last time, thanked everyone for
coming, then off to his little room, and died.

WORD COUNT

*The problem for poets
is to both dance and sing
and yet remain within limits
of language.*
—Stanley Kunitz

Kin we hep ye, colloquially? Colossally?
Lament the anti-myth, theodicy of the morally empty?
Grief triangulated in a war widow's flag?

A heron who stands one-footed, feigning balance
Of the time? Wear an old cavalier jacket, frogged, braided,
Long dried saber pricks of forsaken blood?

Soliloquies of guileless guilt, war's ormolu of cartridge clips?
Hair cut with sheep-shear sharpness, sideburns
Of whetted scars? Bring own fans to textured charters,

Devotees, obsessive, coteries of academicians?
Divide Melville, Conrad, Faulkner from Jacobean tragedy,
Shakespeare, the King James bible?

Granitic jawing of pawing politicians, concinnity of tone:
Screeching, howling, yammering, analogical
murmuring in the bone? Dialogue pungent,

Plangent, antic, transit, tectonic trainers swink the verb?
Spoke by mannered mannequins while Malthus sleeps
With chains on legs, those who guard

The citizenry from temptations of the day,
A twelve-gauge Remington stands at attention
In the comer, a box and a half of shells.

THE TERRORIST

He has a closed-caption voice
running at the bottom
of his silences. The terrorist
sits staring
into darkness of his soul,
a pit of dry dust
emptied of rage, unmartyred,
despairing of life left
meaningless
on earth.

BARABAS, THE BARBER OF TURTLE BEACH

Great white swans drift down
on black peat fields

As Delta salmon spawn in the fall
on the San Joaquin River

Snowgeese, mallards, teal
have had their fill of asparagus

Lumber over tule berms, as Barabas,
the barber, has set up winter shop

In his old houseboat, face chiseled
from briarwood and pickled teak.

He stands behind his fisherman's
fighting chair

Stropping razor as if challenging
the stories yet to come.

THE RAG DOLL OF DAYBREAK

First sun
Color of a pit
In an over-ripe peach
Skizz shazz of sky
Bluer than burnt pewter
In the eyes
Of the rag doll of daybreak
Open and beseeching
Remembering the hugging
Paralyzed with joy.

TAKING THE RED-EYE

Somewhere, on a hidden track of time
there's a train for us: the express, mail train,
slow train
or even the red-eye that crosses fields
of night
secreting sighs of steam in deeper dark
of venous blood, hilarities and jealousies
in houselights pocking out; our last stop
with sleepy city cabbies
lined like racehorses for their jockeys
groomed to race at dawn.

BETWEEN SILENCES IN HAVANA

Light lies gray and even on the sea. Outside
the window the mussel seller's daughter

Wears a string bag of silvery black shells
around her neck. The old woman in the room

Across the hall sits day and night by daguerreotypes
of her dead children. Faint frazzing of time,

Old dance halls of Havana come to life, señoras
singing by their congas, soft voices in Cachimba,

A frothy frottage in darkened rooms by a clientele
of oystermen and goatherds. *Que lindo es sonar*

Despierto, How beautiful it is to dream while

we're awake. Lips with flavor of lime mango,

Traces of a honey liquor the Russians call Medkova
that leaves the long, lingering sweetness of her

Kisses, mouth partly open, breathing silences,
no words more blissful.

CRUISING WITH THE SEALS

When life becomes a Seattle cruise ship
moving stealthily
like a giant white Kodiak bear
with a spawning salmon in its mouth,
bloody smudges where the anchor chain
plunges to subaqueous coldness
of the heart

He stands close to the rail
listening to lectures
infusing soul with mammals, birds, fish,
wrapping himself in ice sheets
of pale blue chiffon, out where absolutes
are sculpted scripture, voice of the lecturer
weaned on outwash & glacial till . . .

The thought of her brings suffocation,
need to surface like a pinniped Wedell seal
after diving a thousand feet or more,
coming up to laughter in the ship's saloon,
mouth on his drink from the steward,
feeling all eyes upon him, his seal's buck teeth
gnawing the ice for air.

I AM SEARCHING FOR MY ISLAND

—to Rebecca B.

I am searching for my *shima* in a rice
    paper sea (ten-stroke ideograph)
for island in Japanese)
    where truth, stripped naked, is
forgiving. I bought a box lunch, prayer
    sticks, an inkstone from the master
of Shoda in Kyoto
who knows his 1,850 characters
as if they were his children.

You will pass horizons, he said,
    deceitful heavens
where sunsets stream bloodlit colors
    seeping through gray gauze bandages
of war. Your island will be a place
    of peace where love will multiply.

My cargo is the master's box of brushes
    I am to burn for him on this island,
an honoring of workmen's tools, he said,
    think of your America: bridles, saddles,
saws, picks, hammers, axes. You will follow
    this seabird I will script;
when the bird tires in flight an island
will rise from the sea to comfort you.

Filled with courage, I can now cross tacks
    with any sailor in the world,
eyes on the faint white wink of feathers
    spiraling down, my *shima* rising
from the sea.

THE BOK BOK MAN

Back when the sternwheeler *Marian Belle*
was called the *Chickee San* in John Wayne's
Blood Alley, the Bok Bok Man patrolled
sleepy streets of the Chinese village of Locke,
pounding on his wooden   bok   bok   *all is well*
all is well

Until one night he saw the first flush of flames
ring Walnut Grove, heard the swarming flight
of terror-stricken herons, sounded the alarm
that saved the Delta village.
At night, in sleepless state, rocking in the wooden
cradle of my boat on Steamboat Slough
I listen to the slap of tide on hull, so much like
bok   bok   bok   bok
time to enter my shrine of sound, listen once again
the Bok Bok Man's   *all is well*
all is well.

KITTY K.

We are thankful
For the wide flared bow
Slicing thin fillets
Of murky rollers,
Our Kitty K., undisturbed,
Curled in sleep
Between diddy bag & washdown hose,
Her tiny nose wrinkled
In kittenish delight, chasing
Her twine-ball dream
Into the mysterious cruise
Of night.

SAILING IN A VAST NEW OCEAN CALLED JOY

There's music
in the orange-flush intimacy of sea
meeting sky, a mauve
movement
by Handel, notes bobbing to the metier
of gray ships on the horizon
as the view from the fo'c'sle narrows
to her unclothed form
carved like a figurehead on a Marblehead
schooner
racing before the wind; she's lying
in the rope pocket below the bowsprit stem
taking her morning shower bath in the prow's
wake, shrieking in the wild glaze
of saltstream like a member of the Furies
as we cross the Tropic of Cancer together
into a vast new ocean called Joy.

VIAGRAIZE

Soon after composing his Yeatsian couplet,

O, Mistress Muse, touch these words both dense
and dumb, viagraize that which is numb—

He felt a tingling in his sensory probe as if a wild
Etruscan woman had given him a shot of
estrus; thinking of a contemporary, Oliver Wendell
Holmes, who said at 93, watching a young lady
walking below his window, 'O, wow, what
wouldn't I give to be 70 once again!'

INTELLECTUAL WARMTH

In the mind's interstellar coldness
    he wanted to savor
her intellectual warmth, stroll beside
    her on sabbatical,
become bibliopegic in the archives,
    flit through pages
one step before her fingers, snuggle
    warmly in her Macintosh
when she slept at night, dance with words
    that reached her lips,
remembering scholarly significance,
    where they came from,
the soft crush of form shaping texture
    of her kiss.

MAXINE'S SHIFT

The waitress wears a durable Max Factor,
color of light sweet crude,
wipes white doughnut dust from counter,
greets each roustabout by name
as they troop in, knows where each man sits,
separate orders: she's mother, sister,
pretend lover, all hungers featured on her menu.
If you miss the tip her smile remains soft,
simpatico, and when Maxine rings up the tab
the parrot who sits in his cage above the cash
register says *cheapskate! cheapskate!*
loudly in Spanish to laughter gathering like
a gusher, where preciousness of humor
strikes deep in everyone.

THE GRABBLIN' MAN OF DE KALB, TEXAS

From the tracks you could see the old man
with white grabblin' scars on black arms,
reach down in the sulfurous river

Near De Kalb, Texas, watch him bring up
a thrashing 100-lb flathead flatfish
from its hidden nesting place,

Arm up to elbow, plunged deep as a rail
spike through the mouth, far into belly;
he'd wave the fish at us like a silver flag

Spangled with sun as we seek air on a flatcar
moving slowly along, marveling at the
triumph of man over hunger, that he

Would be dining tonight as we rolled on.

FRED'S GEKKO

—to Scott W.

through thin apartment walls
you can hear her call her husband

fred, damn you, fred!

her shout to him from another room
is like a voice flipped back
to earth
on a meteor's tail

fred, damn you, fred!

you gotta do something about the damned
cockroaches, fred!

so fred went down to the pet shop
to buy a gekko
to eat all the cockroaches

it wasn't long until

fred, damn you, fred!

when she finds gekko droppings
spread like sesame seeds
on the morning toast

COWRIE SHELLS & BANGKOK PEES

—to Jerry and Sue

He wore a surplus Nato field jacket, Thai earrings,
Berber Cross & Sanskrit ring, UKRAINE BEET FESTIVAL
t-shirt, fake Russian pocket watch, souvenir from Aeroflot,
stone-washed Levis with torn knees.

She wore an enlisted woman's pea coat, double-breasted
with brass buttons, tribal necklace of frosted glass beads,
t-shirt, one side SIBERIA, LAND OF OPPORTUNITY
the other, RUSSIAN WOMEN'S LIB, carried a Nepalese

Knapsack woven in autumn colors. They undressed
together before a tall Peruvian mirror from Lima,
he in Batik boxer shorts hand batiked in Bali.
She wore nothing but a sterling silver turtle locket

With a chiming bell inside that tantalized the hours,
kept ringing the changes of their kisses until he
was out of cowrie shells, paid his debt to her
with gambling chips of Bangkok pees.

YOU ARE THE ROUX IN MY GUMBO

—to Nina

You are the roux in my gumbo, said Gramps,
your invisible dobros add riffs to the spirit,
no pop culture battened down, my little social
heroes with your philanthropy of love!

We gather here before I take the long slow spin
into stone-cold silence; now don't give me
your e-bookish look, you know I'm more than
loquacious, a curiosity beyond blather and ink,

Hoping my psychosis is emollient, disappears
in a fast-food fix. So, we meet at the intersection
of the senses, pluralistic in passions, no need
for affidavits to declare our love, for you speak clearly,

Kiss in the street, while my War-Two generation
can barely remember *The Leaping Libidos*
at the Circus Of Flesh; and with deep regret I confess
that each of you has not lived one day without war,

Plunderer of blood and treasure, admiring still all
troops sworn to keep us safe, while you study words
enmity and *amity,* become doctors of diplomacy,
lubricate tweeky wheels, let rapprochement

Become the song of Peace, for if the chemistry
isn't human, change the formula, for you, dear
children, are the living link of hope that stirs
my endless dream.

TALLEYRAND'S COFFEE

—to Linnaea P.

If you hang out, said father, become
burned in the social solarium,
go to your favorite coffee shop,
put some mocha in your modem—

Order Talleyrand's coffee, they'll
ask you how to make it, tell them what
he said, 'Black as the devil, hot
as hell, sweet as an angel, pure as love'—

Remind them, it's not the way you grind
your beans, essence of its steam, vigor,
ardor of the body, but in honoring
the order, mine is yours, yours is mine,

Let's toast the taste of our coffee man,
Mr. Talleyrand, to peace & joy,
Forevermore!

AT THE BORDER CROSSING
OF THE MIND

—to K.P. S.

I wait behind
the Eunuch of Ennui
at the border crossing of the mind

Ever watchful
for the Assassin of Creative Thought
on furlough

From Grave Robbers International,
whose duty
is to destroy, dismember lines of poetry

That when properly
enjoined
could bring down kings.

ON TOUR WITH THE JEJUNE JUMPING BEANS

—to Glen S.

As sure as sex is a theme park after dark & all roadies
are timorous & tummy-tucked, I toured with a road
company called the *Jejune Jumping Beans,* hip-hopped
across tundras of broken dreams. I did a *pas de deux* with
Madame Bagnio whose wide hips were repositories of
subtle rhythms. I felt nimble as Microsoft Man who wears
vaporwear for underwear, happy to flee the hospital of our
Lady of Suborning Perjury. Our entire cast, in fact, looked
like we were on loan from Madame Tussaud's Wax
Museum. We spoke a secret stichomythia (each speaker
uses one line of verse) an interplay of earthiness, terror of
the times, like our laundry, delicate & cumbersome,
drying on hangers in the bus like the ghost of Banquo
boogyian down the aisle. Our women's leotards were
patched with Dragon's Breath, blouses pinned with
purple cornflowers from Stockholm.

On we traveled, in the blue-beveled night-eye of our
hunger, marking moons around Uranus, vagaries of flesh,
temptations of the mind, so poor we ate sonastina crackers
with *Frijoles En Olla,* beans in the pot at Mexico City;
Glubowski, our stagehand, carried a 1989 Polish Solidarity
sausage in his trunk, quartered a huge onion under the
scrim to quicken our diva's tears. When we parked at night
our driver Demonthenes, who was over-qualified for your
American game called *Jeopardy,* would lure our little
dancers we called *peti-rats* behind the bus's prim canvas
curtain in the back where he would emerge perspiring,
smiling, as if he had successfully changed a tire. As sure as
Volvo means *I go* in Latin, vulva was the catchword
for ancient stage-door johnies who waited & wailed like
rain-drenched cats for the last show's ending, stumbling
about with wilted bouquets, rancid candies, their
incantatory chant for   tu tu's   tu tu's   as if to ease the

rat-dropping numbness of the night. We'd roll on to Oslo, Copenhagen, holding hands with my benefactor, Madame Bagnio, who believed in man's essential goodness while my cynicism glowed in the dark. She tried, dear soul, to coax a churlish serenity out of me as if all were good we'd be invited to the *Marriage Of Figaro* at Lincoln Center in your New York City. She even prayed for me, an abandoned orphan, something no one else had done. "I don't want you to end up like those stagedoor lotharios," she said, "So insufferably lonely—or infuriate a ravening pack of animal spirits who will eat you alive, spit out the bone buttons on your coat." So thanks to Madame Bagnio I've tried to sanitize my soul, light candles instead of fireworks, refuse to visit zoos on afternoons off stage, and practice, ardently, our *pas de deux.*

RUNNING TO THE SUN

—Kamikaze, the Dragon Divers, 1945

I had found my take-home, a Japanese parachute
on a small island off Okinawa, blue-lipped
sea of sound, lacy filigrees of destroyer shells, shrill
as crazed seabirds on the beach beyond.

I'm in a prayer grotto abandoned by villagers, suicides,
whose bones bound grief to faint veins of pain
that swelled & throbbed in Paleozoic stone.
My Marine buddies deciphered the pack's lettering:

> *For my little brother, Okira.*
> *I've been chosen by the Dragon Divers,*
> *our Kamikaze of the Divine Wind;*
> *use it for your prayer-pillow, Okira,*
> *as I have no need of it where I am going.*
> *Think of this honor as our victory.*
> *Pray for me. Kyocho*

War ended. I lugged the chute by LST to Japan,
returned to San Diego where my wife
marked, cut my prize, sewed small dresses
to the delight of our daughter & friends, their
little legs flashed on shadowed silk of laughter,
as if running to the sun.

—Author's note: *I abhor war,*
but love the troops and their families.

SOUNDS I FORGOT TO TELL JACK KEROUAC
ABOUT IN 1952

I'm in an old yellow caboose on the siding,
head resting on a conductor's thin cane satchel
hard as a motel pillow; he's up forward, somewhere,
on duty for six more hours, doesn't know I'm here.

Sleepless sounds of a little all-night switch engine
grunting & goading big freight cars into lines
for unloading the wealth of America; a refrigerator
car droning like a jungle cat sleeping off a full

Stomach, scritchy squeal of steel on steel,
pneumatic woooooooosh of bleeding brakes, shuddering
lock of couplings like giant steel handshakes after
crossing the Continental Divide; here, in the half-

Drowsed heat of Albuquerque, layers of sound, harsh,
heavy, light, piteous as a plash of mother's tears;
it's here I'm appointed conservator of sounds for the
southeast, northwest, eastbound, Rocky Mountains,

The long desert rolls, short stuttering stops of the cities,
backing, fitting, starting, stopping like transient lives;
swinging lanterns of light on the ceiling, timed
to the soft crunching beat in cinders

By the switchmen's boots, all hushed for the moment,
waiting for the final sound, persistence of the engineer's
whistle, the train-cry, coruscations of its call, ring in
the sting of tin-cup morning coffee, picking up your

Bedroll, Jack, and moving on.

CINNAMON AND TANDOORI

She was a moral hazard

    with a sensual scent

Of cinnamon and tandoori,

    blend of bay leaf

And star anise, sweeping stride

    of cloves and curry

Down anointed streets, disdainful

    at stares of admiring men,

As she spit cardamom seeds

    from her teeth at them,

Wives laughing behind

    their curtains.

WAVING GOODBYE TO EL TREN DE LA MUERTE

—to Jane E.

1.
Son, said Gramps, before you get your ticket punched,
sit in the club car splendor of *El Tren de la Muerte,*
leave anger and despair in the baggage car, watch life
unfold beneath the window. Speak softly in an off-stage
voice, bold, do not whisper, listen for a largo beat
on tabla drums, ask the conductor to let you off, not
at some whistle-stop, but a place of *gens de couleur*
where skull & bones wear swallow-tail tuxes, scholarships
in social justice; check your leverage ratio, moral hazards,
pay off the liquidity of tears, not a shrewd investment.

2.
Life is not a six-course dinner from a Petri dish,
be unafraid of political fevers, be proactive, son, carry
on our dna in a non-dimensional way, emblazon
signs of the seasons, stroll the lambent path of
laughter, metabolize your tongue with sweetness,
invent a multiplex persona, gather energy from the
street, un-seed all greed, find a woman with dress
transparent, a style approved by parents, perhaps
a Lydia of mainstream media, someone ready to break
your story before global warming melts it all away.

ROBERTO THE ROBOT

—to Richard K.

I found a robot in the rabble; fields swept
In cadmium, bluish white, as if dusted
With disaster. He appeared surprised
As Zeus who had swooned a swan
In a feather-dusted dance of lust;
His ID unlit, traced to a robotarian
Called Roberto, an escort of celebrity
Who had blown a 1.3 on the metal meter,
A breathalyzer without prejudice as he
Screamed above high-C for missing parts,
Most vulnerable of his valuables, plus
A pheromones detector for his species
Search, la feminine, sadly dismantled,
His audio most guttural, choked on verbs,
Said his bandoleer of bling was stolen.
I felt sorry for Roberto, the piety of his
Passions, after all, he was of humankind
Design, a heavy burden for Roberto who
Rose from Beach-Sweep, First Class,
To a post-modern Valentino; so I ordered
A triage of riveters for a meticulous re-
Assembly, bring back sheen to coppery skin,
This time more radiant, demeanor almost
Spiritual, a new image without a trace of sin.

OVER THE WINTER SEA

At six I rode in the first mourner's car
behind the hearse,
sat on a tip-up seat pressed against granny's
thin hard knees,
both of us missing grandpa terribly,
too mystified by death
to cry, and when we rode over the headland bridge
I thought death
was like the terns stealing fish from the brown
pelican's pouch; felt a little
better as I watched the surfbirds' swiftness
outside the window
as they raced the hearse, passed ahead of us,
veered off, wings spread
like grandpa's playing cards when we played
Fish together, now scattered
over the winter sea.

A GRANDMOTHER'S CHRISTMAS

—to Deborah T.

She was a little simmering teapot
with the scent of cloves and orange peel,
kissing grandchildren of men back
from the big breakers, heavy weather,
family spilling from the small trim social
hall on the finger pier where women
barbecued coho salmon on cedar planks,
fresh aioli sauce, toasts of Glennfiddich
whiskey to those who didn't come back with
tides of the years. Of the sea birds, only
the cormorants, roosting high abeam
of the wind, sleepless, waited for mankind
to kiss the little old sea goddess goodnight,
up early to tar their boats, become partners,
share the sea with them once again.

MARCO POLO SAYING
GOODBYE TO GRANDMOTHER

Grandmother's voice, upon awakening
became a sound
gliding on fins of light, fluttering,
calling to the hunger
of her pet fish, Marco Polo, *cyprinus carpio,*
she tells us children, a carp, spangled
in florescent colors, rising
at dinner time
from the depth of the pond
in which he was born, touched her old
freckled hand for his reward, a resplendent menu
of food and love.
The nurse, gently, after he's been fed, placed
grandmother's hand back under the covers
of a gray afternoon,
as Mr. Polo, we called him, flicked his tail
at death, disappeared
in the water lilies, barely disturbed
the dark green water
beside the dream
that floated endlessly
by her bed.

BLUE IRON
                    —to Karl K.

A photographer I know
is so dedicated to his art, extracts,
for photographic plates, pure albumen from
the eggs of eagles; to catch, he says,
blue iron blazing in the irises—

A piercing vision, far-sighted,
to lead him, unerringly, through darkrooms
of the night to morning sunlight
burning away the fog of rant without reason,
where the world, dressed in new innocence,

Is waiting for its picture.

ROYALTY OF THE RETINA
                    —to Jackson W.

The mind, carpetbagger of the senses,
Back-pack stuffed and streaming

With decisions, inquisitor of the cerebral,
Savant of the sacred, sitting in with the

Eyes of experience, Royalty of the Retina,
A judge of humanity's long parade,

Nobility's mischievous behaviors, a
Reservoir of hope replenished for the

Jobless and despairing, co-mingling with
A spirit in what you give will never end.

REVELATIONS OF THE TWENTY-FIRST

What? Mark Twain wasn't Huckleberry Finn?
Holden Caulfield signed for H.D. Salinger?
We young poets and writers had First
Amendment Rights? All of our creations
Could be observed or ignored?

Life was not a codified embargo paid by
Software of our nights, verisimilitude
Becomes a fiery blend of folklore;
That my dear late grandmother, who could
Break her own saddle stock, had read

The Age of Indiscretion in three languages
Told me about those in her time she
Hadn't cared for, sat sumptuously on hotel
Balconies plumed in ostrich feathers,
Nest of guile and gossip, peering through

Long lorgnettes for the *arrivistes* to arrive,
Be it a 1937 Essex or chauffeured limousine,
All for the whiff of new money, scandal, family
Pedigrees: Wondering what grandmother would
Call the stifling of privacy, a vexing

Of the text-ing, democracy performing stately
Waltzes, rock and rolling, but always reaching out,
Arms around us, a love unvanquished, to be
Shared by one and all today.

WHY OLD MUSICIANS STILL PLAY YOUNG

—to Tami M.

Jazz is the greatest of liberties.
—Anon.

Was it Cervantes who said life is a long-term narrative?
I follow a faint, red-dusted light of old brick buildings,
the trace of city tears down plaster cornices of grief.

I had left a ballroom floor with a revolving ball
of seductive spins, it winked, blinked, for the last
dance of the evening, as we musicians prepared

To pack our instruments. No taxi, I walked to a small
transient hotel that seldom slept, drowsy hum
of a lamentable larvae that turned into resplendent

Butterflies, prepared to die for the beat within them.
Time to bolt the door, prop neck of single chair
under doorknob, un-strap case, scarred, battered from

A delirium of one-night stands, unwrap my treasure,
The Blue Box. Blue Note's Best, wrap hotel towel
around the speaker as if sound possessed;

Opened with Thelonious Monk's *Around Midnight,*
3.09, visualize him weaving over his box
like a black-crowned night heron, surely an endangered

Species endowed with creative genius; followed by
Sonny Rollin's saxophone, *Decision,* 8.01,
A soaring spill, fountains of notes shimmering far beyond

Liner notes in my darkened room; Miles Davis, next,
horn exploring *My Mind, 4.01,* as if it were my own;
can't wait for John Coltrane's *Blue Train, 10.40,*

Shaded tone, remembering Pinetop Perkin's *I can hear
the whistle blow, no train around;* Last respects
to Dexter Gordon's *Don't Explain*, 6.03,

Like a mother's good-night prayer to me, put away
my cache of dreams, return to the chorus
of human energy surging through paper-thin walls,

Lovers whispering, singing springs, a vivacity of sighs,
snores, groans, troublesome sounds, arguing, making-up,
at this I smile, saluting in the dark; Dino's All-Night Diner's

Splash of color, a neon splendor on my window,
late motors ticking over, shouts, goodbyes,
knowing the old bus will be there in the morning,

Waiting, as the world waits for our music, something
they'll never hear, the beat, so personal and persevering,
unless we climb aboard.

CHUBASCO

Before weather turns,
quickly as a tiger shark
eviscerates a green sea turtle,
frigate birds feed close colleagues
in clear mid-air, inquisitive
jacks break surface, feeling
the cruel invasion
of colder water, the shark's fin
disappearing
before a darkening horizon,
gills like a feather boa
stained with turtle blood,
fibrillating
in the last hot sun, as we batten down
the hatches of our lives, turn, once
again, to face the storm.

A LESSON ONLY LOVE HAS TAUGHT
                —to my daughter, Diane

When one has caught the scent of death
in a shuttered room, an open field's
tableau vivant

Of martyred warriors, or a storm so savage
it tears the heart from
a little home,

No pictures saved of family, friends,
an album of the spirit, gone,
a preciousness

Only God bestowed, and love has taught.

BEALE STREET JUG BAND: PORT Of MEMPHIS

—to Nathan S.

Once in the 50's I waited to board Memphis Queen II
at the port of Memphis, listened to the Basin Street
Jug Band beating a bright rococo rhythm,

The captain & engineer leaned over the wheelhouse,
laughing & clapping; Suddenly I knew it was going
to be a happy voyage, frisky jug beat blowing,

Nipping heels up the gangway, jazzing my ju ju
juices for New Orleans reclining like a sultry woman
on satin pillows, waiting down the river of the mind.

THE LORD EXECUTIONER OF TRINIDAD

At the Lenten Festival in Trinidad
fishermen were patching souls of their boats,
Kings of Calypso reigned; Lord Executioner, Growler,
Attila the Hun, Black Prince, The Mighty Sparrow,
mothers ironing uniforms in their kitchens.
Lord Executioner said, 'What is more priceless
than a brother or a sister? True, mon, look
what I found in this morning's paper, some trivia
from the treasury of Uncle Sam. Do you know
that my little brother who weighs one hundred eleven
pounds is the same as a million dollars in twenty-
dollar bills?'

DOS GARDENIAS

If you've worked night shift in a sugar mill,
said Samuel, you'll not believe
the old folk tale concerning Cubans:
that we spend all day shopping for chickens
and all night in our bedrooms where we
become sexually heroic. Come with me in my
enchanting old Chevrolet Impala, I'll take
you to hear my friends of the Buena Vista Social
Club play 'Chan Chan', 'El Quarto de Tula',
'Dos Gardenias', then you'll say, music
makes us brothers and sisters of the world,
forbidden to fight as rhythm unfolds
the enticing mystery of our lives, where
Peace, himself, plays the tamba, invites all
dancers to the floor.

TANGO TANDA
                 —Milonga salon, Nino Bien,
                 Buenos Aires, Argentina

I advise the loneliest man in the world
To become brave as a *gaucho*,
Take a *salida*, entrance step of the tango,
Walk down a line of jacaranda trees
To the district *Carrientes*, find music
Of a *milonga*, tango salon, table for two
By the dance floor, sign for Argentina's
Intimate *tanda*, series of four themed-alike
Tangos; So please tell me, after dancing
Together for 15 minutes, you've found
Partner a stranger, when both of you
Brought closer in this bitter old world,
Tango's warmth thrumming in your veins.

MR. TORGERSEN

A man's face is his autobiography
        —Oscar Wilde

Mr. Torgersen looked tough as a Hammerhead turtle
sitting on his front porch waiting for his paper,
dour, spitting and clawing for breath,

Gave me such bad looks I almost fell off my bike
until I solved his congeniality problem,
as mother said;

So I double-cuffed his morning paper, hummed
A tisket, A tasket, Ella Fitzgerald's song
of the day, threw it straight

Into Mr. Torgersen's little yellow basket
strung between two big oxygen tanks
that stood like palace guards

Protecting the old man from our exasperated
town. And from then on Ol' Turtle,
as we kids called him, threw me high-fives,

As we would call them now, and radiant smiles
that brightened my collections
as time sped on.

POLISHING THE SILVER

At seventeen in my small coast town
dawn was diaphanous with hope.
My first job was on the fish racks, sting
of cold bay-water on blueberry field
scratches, the old wooden bay dock
swaying like an older woman coaxing
you to dance over the white-spotted
winks of shore bird droppings as we
chummed first with rock cod carcasses,
luring fresh cod to feast on their brothers'
bones, not unlike our present swarm of
polished silver protein escaping upstream
against the tide.

EXODUS TO PARADISE

—to Rosemary W.

I awake to the channel of thought,
bright blaze over water,
watching the last gray whales
migrate down the coast.
They nod silently, as if inviting me
to join an exodus to paradise.
I wave back, knowing they are going
to Mexico's winter shelter,
yet wonder, will I be here to greet
my silver shrouded friends
on their return?

OLD PAINT

—to Dean and Donna

Grand'pa, a widower, was proud of his American
quarter horse, Old Paint, a big 16-hand gelding,
color of strawberry fields on foggy Oregon mornings;
led by grand'pa to the pump-shelf after breakfast
as he washed a giant cast-iron skillet, cups, dishes,
talked softly to Old Paint as he'd been taught as
a boy by his American Indian friends, true to
an old truth he lived by, *Know where you want
to go without leaving behind where you came from* ....

Old Paint would nicker, stomp foreleg hoof, eager
for the long ride from ranch to post-office
where his master would show off his Paint,
a bright flag of living horseflesh to the town folk,
but the horse always knew, in the transition of
feelings between horse and man, that much
depended on the mail, how his master sat
in the saddle when he had read big, black-lined
letters from the War Department, two sons,

John and Ted, Master Sergeant and PFC ....
it was then, without touch of rein, Old Paint knew
it was time for him to turn around and head for home.

ROAN IN THE RAIN

The boy's horse stands against the wind,
rump wet with rain,
opalescent pools gather on its withers,
stream down fetlock to upheld hoof
stamping three times for recognition—

Something important was happening
in their lives, as the young master
steps into the bus for his first day of school,
as if any boy saying goodbye to his horse
is turning into a man—

Waving from a back window, remembering
everything through the years, sheen
of its bay colored coat, touches of gray and white,
the big eyes, imploring, waiting by the fence-line
in the rain for his return.

—Author's note:

As New Viking is celebrating the 50th Anniversary of the counterculture classic, *On The Road* by Jack Kerouac, a rite-of-passage best selling novel in 1957, I remember, after War Two, around 1952, I lived in Acuitlapan, a small Mexican village between Taxco and Cuemevaca. On weekends I would catch a ride into Mexico City to visit fellow American writers and see Jack Kerouac who, I believe, was writing *Mexico City Blues* at the time. Little did I know that his 120-foot-long scroll manuscript he kept pasted together for his typewriter would sell years later for 1.4 million at a Sotheby's auction or be an inspiration for everyone from Bob Dylan to the Beastie Boys. The last part of the novel had been chewed by a neighbor's dog and had to be re-written, outside of that published as written, Sal Paradise as Jack Kerouac and Dean Moriarty, his friend and confident, Jack Cassady, his driver. The book still sells today, a college syllabus backpack special, as young people have a continuing interest for 'the open road' despite literary scholars and critics calling the text overly-romantic with a flowery exuberance, but nevertheless, Kerouac was writing what he was thinking at the time, broke a few rules, but still a valuable cultural influence as his archives flourish.

THE DANCING DAUGHTER OF
THE BUTCHER DE TORO

*It is not the same to talk of bulls
as to be in the bullring.*
—old Spanish proverb

About the time in 1952 Jack Kerouac was in Mexico City
writing *Mexico City Blues*
I was also there, restless as a salamander in the *sambra*,
shady side of the bullring in that resplendently
mordant city, feeling my way down this ancient wooden
structure
swaying with olés from the toreadors' passes, swirling
veronicas, coming down to the netherworld
of this hellish rotunda like an armadillo dazed
on cheap tequila

Down, down, under the stands moaning with manflesh
and womanflesh
to a long line of poor holding out pesos for dewlaps
and quarters from a freshly killed bull
drug in by two donkeys who stood bored in their traces,
flies humming about ears sticking from woven straw hats,
whimsical, comical, but for the Butcher de Toro
slashing sinews and shadows
with a razor-sharp machete dripping red from the meat
as his daughter entertains, dancing in her black

Patent leather slippers over a carpet of the bull's dark
blood, her eyes fixed on this dissolute gringo
with a kind of pity as I stumbled about without showing
a peso, as if nothing she or her father could do
to assuage my hunger, not even the bull's head,
proper cradle for menudo to appease the sick and starving,
the bull's eyes open, unblinking to the torment of
the flies, staring at me like the dancing daughter
of the Butcher de Toro long after I had gone
to the cantina, look in the bar mirror, swear to myself
I was still alive.

WHERE SHE WAITS FOR ME

Are those wisps of cloud, a gauzy voile

hiding the beauty of her face?

Does the tide's blue tulle reflect remembrance

as I drift beyond the breakwater

of my heart to an open sea,

far from distant barking of the

harbor seals

sunning on private buoys, insolence

of their rocking sleep

while I must stay awake, steer by mysterious

variations

found in the truth of glass, to where, garlanded

by rainbows, she waits for me.

RAY'S RAP 2: XC

Everything has been said
but not everyone has said it.
                                    —Anon.

O, what time has wrought! Dissing dots on an
ocelot,   Yo, let's bond like orcas in a pond,
A Bono & Sting sing-along.   Alienated?
Time to play,   At the Internet Café,
All evolving, not dissolving,   Conceptualize
the mind's surprise,   A cosmos of disparate souls,
Who remain absent at the polls,   The importune
stay out of tune,   Do what musicians do,
Only the young outlive *The Who,*   No rude
dude without cachet,   Brings down the day,
A power couple who lost their purse   To assuage
a lobbyist's thirst,   An analogy of blood & bone,
disappearing into stone,   Please store wisdom
From the Gray Hairs,   Save yourself real life's
despairs,   Of all steamy synergies,   Sex reclaims
its energies,   A low carbon economy,   Is a climate
changing nominee,   An odyssey of solar, wind,
bio-diesel,   Worthy of an artist's easel,   All posted
on a take-down list,   Reputations seldom missed,
The more we talk,   The less we say,   Excesses
of the day,   Language, appearing antic, becomes
charismatic,   Mother earth's swollen nipples,
May hide clean coal tipples,   Beware those who've lied,
Steal remnants of your pride,   Pause to laugh
at paragraphs,   Shocks inter-netting staff,   Short term
complexities,   Sedates the culprit of our needs,
Liberty does not come free,   Installments paid by you
and me,   Take courage on the cusp of candor,   Take
no senseless slander,   A bastard's brio caught in shame,
has earned his name,   Be loyal to a gentle code,
Honor love's mother-lode,   Use reportage with noble
zeal,   All we hear, see & feel,   For we are the last tribe
with pen,   Assuring grace of peace,   Will come again.

WITH CLARA AND CHARLIE AT TIKI LAGUN

—Northern California Delta

We turn southwest of light 24 to Lost Isle,
one mile up to Turner Cut, enter Tiki Lagun,

Welcomed by two mascot goats, Clara Bow

and Charlie Chaplin who delight in butting us

Down the mooring float because we forgot
their sugar cubes. After our breakfast

Of Rancho Huevos with tiny shots of tequila,
the chef gives us little packets of sweetness

For Clara and Charlie who face us, heads down,
eyes up, on the ramp. They are waiting

For our passports before official clearance
to the sun-spangled glory of the San Joaquin.

CAP SKAGG'S LAST VOYAGE

Ol' Cap Skaggs lived alone on his ancient
San Francisco tug
on Little Potato Slough in the Delta, moored to a Chinese
elm near the Chinese city of Locke, close to his favorite
bar & café, Al-the-Wop's. Ol Cap's a hero at Herman &
Helens, fellow river-rats along the thousand miles
of inland waters, his quick smile like a silvery half-scoop
of live bait, remembered fondly by tourist boaters
he rescued from islands of Delta peat; traded long ago
his marine radio for a Rudy Vallée megaphone; received
bad news from the clinic,
classic good form, told everyone it was nothing,
just a mild, mid-summer fever—
one last voyage was his decision—
alone, no deckhands off Deep Reef to help with a second
rod when the big fish got too ornery,
a three-hootchie rig for anything that swims,
down waterways of the San Joaquin, waving to everyone,
even monohullers, ragtops with get-home
bow chasers, big cats wind-vaning across his tracks
with awesome wake, on, through The Gate,
to his fresh & open sea, chasing silvers, kings,
remembering his life at sea, nasty storms, 60-knot winds
off Tortola in the Lesser Antilles; time now
to chase ocean perch, thrilled at the eagerness to see
old friends—
captain of the *Hilo Cat* at Morro Bay, on to Double Point,
Marin coast. So what, like everyone else—
out of provisions, fuel—
he would find an end-tie on God's own pier,
call mates over, break out the *Heineken*, toast the miracle,
that all were here.

BALLROOM OF THE SLOW DANCERS

The old man has questions: the young musician
    listens: 'Must I go to the ballroom of slow dancers
    across the street from the old folks' home?

Disappear in shadows of muscle tone?
    Put on Muddy Water's 'The Chess Box'
    where I keep my pretty woman's ring?

Remember Johnny Winter's 'All The Way Crazy,'
    find my book's not bound in leather,
    paper words fade away to brush strokes

From Time's drummer, ticking my life away?'

STRANGER IN THE WIND

He slept with a long bore Winchester wrapped
   in ragged clothes: Eat what you kill, he shouted,
Drink for your thirst, fuck what you will if the
   respondent lends support!

      We were clacketing across East Texas
      in the wind-whipped open door
      of an empty cattle car. I had my trusty
      notebook fitted in shirt pocket denim like
      a small Derringer of truth questioning
      my bewilderment of the options to survival.

It was then he spied my stub of pencil, the death
   of dialogue. If you are connecting words of a life
never lived, he said, I do not authorize its print,
   for I have served time in a dozen personas …

      I could hear the clicked-off safety as he
      unwrapped his rifle, immense relief as he shot
      randomly at prairie dogs in the yellow sand
      whirling beyond our vision, my words hidden
      deep inside me, cautious to this day.

QUORUM CALL FROM A DISTANT MALL

Hell is other people at breakfast.
—Sartre

If bio-ethics are aesthetic, take your peers
To cryotherapy classes in frozen tears;
Self-image is but incautious spillage;
Riff-rockin' rhythm is fusion's vision;
Websites spun in tokes of sun;
A 3G gizzer has no trigger; Give a
Gigabyte for one food-fight;
Nuance is ensconced, a viral spiral
In denial; Elliptical lines strain the divine;
Mr. Font's not one to flaunt; Appear keen

    For genuflected gene, Campy sci-fi,
    Tarzan buff, the real stuff; Testosterone
    Will long be gone; Trolls of night are in full
    Flight, hot pursuit of the hirsute; Men are
    Party trippers with zeitgeist zippers;
    Women ululating during mating; Campaign
    Mode is the mother-load; Time to observe
    Her killer curves, drop-dead divas in peep-toe
    Booties shop for boy-toys in trad-fad cubies;
    Clichés screaming, media keening, hybrid-

Cars over-weening; Neutro-robotic no longer
Exotic; Say fini to extravagant genie; An epilogue
Cum laude fraud; Intransigent gents rule parliament,
But please remember this November, under no
Condition mess with a toxic politician.

CHECKER IN THE GREEN ROBE

Could we check out a barcode
On our ribcage
To judge limits of our hunger?

Stroke syntax of our bar-tabs
To mollify bereavement?
Pull up pants-legs, give warning

When ice-melt seas rise a global 1.5?
Count pixels in the thermals
As life's visuals begin to burn?

For we must sit together at earth's
Graduation picture, and in our
Greenest robes, besides.

PANAMA SONG

—to the late William Willis,
circumnavigator

The night's hot stars spackle darkness
as if shot from scatter guns; water taxis
picking up sots sobering on the beaches.
Smell the salt ocean on top of the hemisphere,
listen to slurrous slap of silt rusting mold-green
walls that pierce the Continental Divide,
the Zone's reconstituted rhythms, sun rising
on the Pacific setting over the Atlantic,
global patois drifting down cobbled streets,
swirling over red-tiled roofs. Your one-day fifty-
dollar pay as a line-handler on the Miraflore's
three flights of locks bleeds down the glass
of a Cuba Libre, the bonus bus pass back to the
free port city of Colon, stolen from shirt pocket,
hands raw from tossing, tying, releasing wet
ropes tied to the dreams of travelers.
This is when you know, old friend, it's time
to go again.

SHARK-SCREAM: SILENCE OF THE SEA

I cherish curiosity as a medicine
of life: I lie beside my surfboard
in the dune grass, silent as a croc

In the night, lured by reddish glow
of an oil-drum fire, intricate dance of
machetes in half-light. I see a panga

Drawn to surf-line with two small
6' sharks bound in fisherman's net.
It was later, to my shame and remorse,

That I'd witnessed, without protest,
a finning of sharks, prized as a soup
in Eastern cultures, as if no one

Had translated Darwin's 'Origin of the
Species' that kept me awake at night.

THE TOWN HALL MEETING OF THE MINDS

I'm caught
in the audiocast webbing
without a metallic spider to spin
its moral: no lurid illuminations, coded
shibboleths of shame, nuances
of the vine

No conscience spared,
we must appear
at the public
bathhouse
for cleansing, scoured, emptied,
prepare ourselves

For the town hall meeting of the minds.

EDITH WHARTON COULD ONLY WRITE IN BED

Dear friends of active verb & sturdy noun,
I salute your selective silences, neither specious

Or sullen, lessons of alliteration, the way you
soliloquize the senses, permitting creation

To be born; flit of assonance, dissonance,
the good juju of enjambment, the traveling man

Of line & couplet; you never starve imagination,
a *ménage a trois* becomes a *Tolkien* trilogy &

When production falls, it's said, remember why
Mr. Longfellow came to call on the novelist

Edith Wharton, his inspiration, who always wrote
in bed.

RECESS

—to Joyce S.

He's down there, somewhere in the subconscious swirl—
No street signs in the subdivision of the mind—

Waiting in pale fluids of amniotic clouds for a poem
To be born, disentangle a ganglia of geekerata—

Knowing this day is for celebration, ponder sweet wonder
Of the invitation, yes, right here in the fount of Socratic

Thought: *The unexplained life is not worth living!*
Small print, no breakdown on company time, excuses,

Doctor's chits, neurological cramps, must face the day,
Inquiry of peers—after all, didn't T.S. Eliot say

What life have you if you live not life together?
Remembering Eavan Boland, *Poetry begins where the*

Certainties end. Here they are, a dazzling display of disciplines
Who wait quietly, kindly, without inquisitorial venom,

A kindred affection, perhaps to find an enormity of emptiness,
Amorphous, vaporous, nothing left but old shibboleths,

Memories of wars and pain; O, those good *citoyens*,
Ductile touch, pat down wooly linings of an old poet's

Threads, thirsty drought, no tinkling coins of wisdom,
Deposit for the knowledge bank of doubt that ingests, aids

The overdrawn. Does he represent the shabby cat of poesy,
Arched back of privacy, purring in rain-dark interludes,

Brain wires formed of fishbones scattered on life's cerebral

Floor, for he's no guru whose reflections are in the eyes

Of Shiva, and what Sheba would want him as a pet, this bloke
Is broke, no transfers freshly minted, no group therapy

To cure Yankee dollars throttled by the bully euros,
No money changers, dour and sour, stock certificates

Turned confetti, scavengers of the sweated poor, gamble
On hydrogen in lieu of filthy Madame Gasolina,

The stripper of *dineros,* scourge of the commuting, as if
Donne, Herrick, Shakespeare are hitching rides

To distant stars; believe Lord Boswell, *Be happy as you can?*
Could there not be an intelligent mischief with an Italian

Pinch of fun? Could he get away with it, poems hidden
In his hamper, no largesse of wit authorized by the witless,

Bon mots rubber stamped and worthless? So please forgive
This old poet fool, cut on his own barbed aphorisms,

Entranced by rogue rhythms, driven, as time uncovers
Brighter days, a discourse that discovers knowledge

As the answer to restless recesses on the playground
Of the mind.

MAKING LOVE TO A STRANGER

This ethereal phrase is not the ellipsis
Of sexual elegance, partied with élan

By college lit classes, fomenting time,
Old wine of social semantics; a daring

Dalliance, imploring flirtation to lose logic,
Becomes a language of the loveliest spoken,

A voice within us inviting the stranger to
Our room where loneliness lingers,

Turns tear-wet pages with the words we've
Missed, so transformation, reborn,

Can begin again.

SONGS OF THE SALMON RIVER CROSSING

—to Kev C.

They peer through wind-torn cowhide
with branding-iron eyes,
reddish rims lashed in winter's light,
horses that tasted air scented with darkness,
careful descent down snaky stream shale to the Salmon
Bar Crossing, teeth chattering like the telegrapher's
keys at the railhead station by the stockyards
east of town—

A brotherly bondage, remembering last summer,
bare-assed in the saddle, laughing, splashing
in cool water, watched by an audience of deer, stately
in silence, blended to brush of their drinking
trail, does who taught young first lessons of fear;
nursed, then, rope-burn hands inured to the ride, cut,
gnarled by the herd; strays found deep in snow,
impaled in barbed wire, eyes open,

Accusingly, ribs thin as split kindling from chunks
by the bunkhouse chinked in creek clay;
guarded freight wagons, prize baking powder, barrels
of flour, far from gambling snaps, whiskey mills,
men who made good money, $50 monthly, three-squares-
a-day, as long as you're single; sure as cookie
boiled venison with root of the callus, kettles
hung by the springhouse, 160-acres, filed public lands—

Saturday nights, rigs from miles around, a little band,
banjo, fiddles, grandpa drummed on a five-gallon
coal-oil tin, sound hollowed thin near the spout,
squeezed out all loneliness, some cowboy man
had left within.

RAILROAD TIME

—Central-Pacific, 1867

Snowdrift covered the tunnel face,
buff-tail deer appeared in powdery mist,
as if on guard, halting the spike-crew's
three-mile track in a 12-hour day.

The powder team doffed leather caps,
stood by fault-holes, crew felled a sturdy oak,
venerable wood for a cross-tie to lay
great-grandfather on. His two best friends,

Engineer and oiler, placed big railroad
watches on his eyelids, as if shelter from nitro-
liquid blasts that shattered the stone of death,
stirred spike-bells to ring the vespers

To carry great-grandad home.

COMING HOME

If words are symbols of a heart that sings
songs of coming home; to walk again under
canopy of trees, old-growth groves
of memory where leaves
dance *en flagrante* in the wind,
drop bright scarves of color warming
the South Santiam River
where deer carved drinking trails
beside dozer tracks tatting the earth
with ugly scars, yet sustained
a good logger like Olle, put food on the
family table—
I can still see him in a forest of firs
and cedar, climbing up, up,
logger spurs jingling, a time before
foot strap, waist, leg harness,
short sharp axe severing limbs like an
acrobat at the Cirque de Soleil,
triumphant tree-topping, saluting Stockholm,
waving at us kids, cut hand-holds,
performing a hand-stand, coming quickly down
to mother's prize, an Oregon berry pie
hot from her kitchen, the same
wondrous smell
I'm coming for today.

THE CHINOOK FROM CENTRAL OREGON

Casting a spell of spangled light
the chinook salmon beats hard on the bank
of the Deschutes River—
this fish, says grandfather, is like my horse—
heavy in shoulder, deep in girth . . .

He counts steely bright scales like rings of age
on a valley oak—reading lifelines—
eleven, fry stage (parr) to smolt—
tells me when it wore its farewell dress
of silver, how long it fed upon the sea,
its long fight back up the Columbia River
locked in to the sweet scent of home . . .

He talks of the salmon's colorations, pink flanks,
dark to muddy red, points to rubicious
body scars
tarnished by water wheels, ladders, concrete vaults,
the burnished burns
of nets . . .

He shows me a gravelly bed where incubation
of the egg occurred, subsisting in umbilical sack—
it is then when grandfather's back is turned

I spear out of the rapids with a stick

the shimmering latex of a condom caught in the eye

of a six-pack ring.

MY WINDOW

I hear a tremoring,
    small stubbled wings
Beneath my window—

A Red-Tail hawk trapped
    a baby starling,
Its small eyes on me, pleading—

All over in an instant, I'm left
    with a bloody smear
On glass, as if the world is my

    window, shut tight
Against pain.

AMERIKA

—for William Willis

in semidarkness he prised a ratguard off a bow hawser,
slid down the line to freedom: Galveston,
Gulf of Mexico, low plains of Texas white with cotton;
secret melding with the workers, grime of a coal passer
darkened skin;
slipping inland, feeling trees in the Brazos Bottom,
land of red-eyed dogs & soft-eyed llamas—
on to the oil fields of West Texas—Oklahoma—
girls with skin like stretch of stars
stitching the states together,
hair curled dark as freighter smoke, burning feather
on the horizon of his desire;
older women who drank straight from the bottle,
men with the lost hope of barroom brawlers, slick splat
of blood, hands balled to fist or glass . . .

remembering lines from Philip Larkin:
I work all day, and get half-drunk
        at night.
Waking at four to soundless dark,
        I stood.

wondering where Larkin found the first lines of the
delta blues in a London park

as he searched now for the fount of this strange music,
face dimetered with hope & disgust, disquieting
dream
awakened to nightmare: pushing up the visored cap
in a stare-down with a boss whose cold eyes
dishumed his humours—
nothing in the dime novels of Buffalo Bill & Texas Jack
rang bells of truth,
so strange in the low German voice of his grandfather

with dreams of *America,* handed down
to become his father's dream
spilling over stone quays, hand winches, liner funnels,
tooting & shrieking of lighters, barges,
steamer cargoes—oranges from Spain, pineapples, bananas,
coffee from Brazil, dried fish
from Scandinavia,
nitrate from Chile; but always the rounding ring of
AMERIKA
his father sticking fuel & water tanks of hobo freighters
like poking holes in the world
to find the rise & fall of a single name,
amerika   amerika . . .
a father lost as his father in deep whoring feather-
beds, drowning in feathered
breast, soft as eiderdown, soft
as a hum, *amerika*—
seabags packed with self-deception, hardtack &
stale tea
lost among those who lie in narrow bunks & dream
of coffins; his grandfather, first,
deck boy on an English ship, four-masted bark
of three-thousand tons,
he, who felt the land breeze of Hamburg without
mal du pays,
nose sharp as a shipwright's axe, big wallowing man,
dancer & roller,
a shouter mixing doldrum's calm,
rumming the song-starved night, shirtfront like a
mainsail
blown out of the boltropes of his belly, a father
who stood on the hot steel deck of a Peruvian guano
carrier
like a big fish with a hook-torn jaw
singing *amerika, amerika . . .*
had he not seen their frigate birds black as crosses
in scabrous sky,
lived, as they had, on raw rye flour from the Andes,
hardtack broken up with belaying pins,

had he not jumped ship for them warmed by a word
liberty
with its hot little belly like a primus stove
simmering his blood?
to this moment as he waits for the American girl
gliding toward him down the bar,
breasts threaded in ropes of Irish linen,
thin dress billowing under the furious wooden fan
like sails of Egyptian cotton . . .

outside, the ravenous sea nibbles at the Narrows,
hoot & shout of sailors pulling at her arms, her dress,
& still she comes to him with outstretched
arms . . . *amerika* . . . *amerika* . . .

Originally published in The Beloit Poetry Journal

KEY LIME PIE

He sits down to a rich cultural menu of menudo
& Dos Equis beer in a little chili cafe hidden
in dunes & sea oats with a blackboard menu that
changes with the cooks. He listens to Tampa Red's
Hokum Band wondering if it's his hangover or Tampa
Red has added a *guitéron* to kazoo & guitar; but all
sound seems to meld melodiously with female laughter
& the whir of the grease-trap fan & the shrimpers'
cosmic head-down appetites ending with a chorus
of Darbukka toothpick percussion. Outside the window
shrimp are running & kids are playing on the public
dock where brown pelicans wait for hand-outs from
the tourists & he's thinking of a yesteryear when
smugglers pushed madeira & put claret out of business
& he's wondering if the smile of the waitress is sincere
as his slice of home-made key lime pie as he points out
to her the antics of a Luna Moth trying to mate on the
ceiling with a Monarch butterfly.

SERENADE: SOUTH OF THE GULF

Pomade glistens
on the hairline
of his lyrics.

He holds the mic
like a scepter
of the gods

Studies distance
between reaction
and resistance

As his woman
dances with *turista*
who throw dollars

Like confetti
to the wind.

CANNONBALL ADDERLEY

—for Michael C. Ford

Upon hearing his name
you thought of war's
                       desolations,
but those who listened carefully, be it Paris
or a jazz joint in Kansas City,
heard a soaring sound
of peace & love, snapping of fingers
in the dark, until first light
                             of dawn,
as Cannonball blessed one & all with the wand
of his alto saxophone.

LUCK OF THE IGUANA

As sure as the iguana
brings us good luck
as we step off the bus
in star-weed & pampas grass,
its life spared, un-splattered
on life's highway—

Entices ears of us old musicians
to recapture the rhythmic
rock of the double-cutaway, semi-
acoustic Kay guitar, two polished necks
streaming an ether of broken frets,
shadow tones burnt deep in bone,

Locked in iguana luck, as age & youth
sit in, playing together,
once again.

PO' MONKEY'S LOUNGE

—to Rich W.

The old dirt road off Highway 61 was thin as the old
man's blood; he breathed hard, slight cough, determined

To take me to the sultry sounds of Willie Seabury's
Po' Monkey's Lounge, where his people danced

To the Mississippi juke house blues. They know me, he said
with pride, never fail to play my favorite *Shim-ee-sha-wobble*

Of the twenties . . . all the girls lined up to partner me . . .
young dudes put on moves to vex rivals . . .

Impress their women . . . I felt an evolutionary beat,
accelerando held down to a blues beat discipline,

A slow enduring movement, hands on undulating flesh
as if hanging on to life itself, a human rhythm

Far beyond the merange and tarantella, the Charleston,
cabbage patch, two-step jerk, Watusi twist,

Fandango, garba, hopa, the Harlem shakes—
samba, salsa, rumba, mambo—

Far past my parent's tango that some say could
both break and heal your heart, *the dancer's world*

is the heart of man, said Martha Graham. I wish Martha
could have been there then, watch the old man's suspenders

Moving slowly with the dance.

BENJY, THE PIANO MAN

Benjamin, the old piano man
sits in a straight-back chair
at the rest home
like a sideman in a traveling bus
booked far into the great beyond.
Benjy's ten-note span hands
once sped over miles of ivory blacks
and tans, smoke-dark keys,
fantasies of a thousand one-night stands;
delicacy of touch lost in orange
and brown melanin
sprinkled over bone and sinew,
hands inert, folded in lap, once a child's
fingers trailing cool waters
of the Bayou La Fouche
as he rode in back of his father's rowboat
to the big house above the levee
where he worked.
Now, his hands have gingerish freckles,
slight tic Souloreux, stills, uncurls,
come slowly to life
when the little girl visits with her mother,
places her kitten in his lap.
Benjy strokes its soft fur as if playing
an old jazz version
of *Kitten On The Keys*, looks up at the nurse
and laughs.

INSTRUMENTAL

—for Nathan S.

I can't remember their names—
but never forgot the instrumentation.
A pick-up band, Portland, Oregon, who ran
the table of sound—
dark water flowing under pilings of old
Willamette Park, dancers' laughter,
a slim young man with a Gibson E5 355
he treated like a little brother,
band-mates, one with a vintage 1954 Telecaster
he would not leave alone on the stand;
a third changing a string on his Gibson Melody Maker
like a young father changing a diaper;
a tall, thin older man, black as his Fender Jazz bass,
who stroked, with a loving slap, eyes half-
closed, humming with the melody—
we left the gig, strangers no longer, zipped,
snapped away our treasures
that have rarely seen the light of day, tucked
away in rooms of small hotels,
waiting for their masters' voices
when they can come out and play again.

QUESTIONS IN CHROME AND YELLOW

—for Jason and Cindy

I'm thinking that my life
could be explained, perhaps,
by a simple dry-print etching.
Who is this amateur dauber
without credentials
sitting at my easel, stealing
sunrises, spoiling profiles,
choking me with linseed oil,
spreading my death without permission
in chrome and yellow?
Why am I to hang in the Louvre,
miscreant of the Absurdists,
admired by courtesans
of soap and water, a voluptuary
with canvas skin
when I could ennoble walls
of the *Musée D'Orsay*
on a fine Spring morning
basking in Parisian light
where there is, like me, no other?

AT THE MOE GREEN POETRY SHOW
NEAR ALVARADO IN WEST L.A.

—The place: Mama's Hot Tamales Café,
1124 West 7th Street,
Los Angeles, California
Rafael FJ Alvarado, Host

The old man thinks he's an oenophile, screw-top poet
on parole, breathing lacy rings of bio-diesel
from rusty throats of city busses—

On a concrete bench near Alvarado, sun blistering
open-toe *haraches,* listening to an ancient Doo-Wop band
from an open window, must be grandfathers

Of funky Hip-Hop kids playing on the corner,
wondering where El Lobos is, a band
that could take a punch or two—

Remembering Moe's early sign-up line, be lucky
one of seven, special tamale ordered
from Mama's hot *cocina*—

Applaud the headliners, so damn good, spread his
long poem flat, words burning on butcher
paper, read something

They had never heard before, hoping young people
were hungry as he is, share whatever's left
on life's table.

IN THE ODYSSEY OF FORGOTTEN TIME

Body language
writhing like smoke
from a Beijing *Big Chicken* cigarette

Staring at the rat-scarred walls of war, detached,
dire dread of the disconnect, as if lisping
Chinese Mandarin in Brooklynese

Technology's swollen throat
spitting out the ravishment of rubbish, feeling
the world growing cold

As the ice woman dancing at the Kirov
to a nocturne by Grieg, audience frozen in polite
applause that melts away with time.

DARK AGE ARISING

Not since the Ice Age blew cold farewell kisses
through a vaporous veil
to beaten down weathermen who had shared
the excesses of her bed, this daughter
of weatherly disorder had
turned into a howling slattern, a phenomenon
of Dark Age Arising, who sang ragged
songs on the Richter Scale,
conspired with her lover who wore striped
carbon dioxide trousers, peered down
from a hole in the oxide layer
at the geothermal gaol
where their faces were posted by *citoyens*
of the planet
for the tricking of temperatures, Anchorage
for Miami, raising sea levels
to tempt the Tsunamis, shot for stoking fires
of global warming, careless burning
of fossil fuels—
Now, on honeymoon—
un-chastened by conscience, incredible pyres
of body-heat, throwing sheets of fire
from hotel windows—incendiary swoon
of a harvest moon—charred filaments drifting down
on a world that never sleeps.

BETWEEN MOMENTS OF REAL FEAR

Between moments of real fear I jump in the pit with my
bongo, let the music take its bites. I believe in the alchemy
of mixing—Hip Hop, Jazz, Chinese, African—I shake them
in a big silver bag with bells, triangles, maracas
saying to myself if music is the art of sound and time I will
borrow my neighbor's Puerto Rican *vejiagante* mask, his
brother the bongo player's orange satin shirt, pretend I can
play the synthesized marimba, sip on a Fresca that turns
into a Rum Surprise, handle my glass like a machete cutting
cane. I will find a woman dark as barwell Jamaican with
big loop earrings, platform shoes, forgetting macaronis are
shooting Columbians in the street below my window where
green neon writhes like jungle pythons and the street-cleaner's
blue chin-whiskered brush scours the tender skin of night.
I will not sit here in my room like a suckered tourist,
a non-smoker with a carton of Duty Free! hating taste of the
fifty-buck champagne—yes—I will play cocktail piano
under pink spotlight dressed in shiny tux stitched with a
hundred Top Forty Charts, between every set I'll draw
workmen's comp, spoil my woman with cut-glass rings—
we'll order send-out food—no pork and bananas, black beans
printed on a plastic menu—real PR beach-shack *alcopurias,*
pastiles, piannonas—we will share *asopao de pollo,*
chicken stew with rice, lips touching on a big wooden spoon.
I will change the woman's politics, remove her black and gold
cammies, take off white cotton panties with the blue Jockey
label, raise her arms, pull down a black cocktail dress
shivering like latex protecting the dark; gently remove her
paratrooper boots, slip on the six-inch glitter spikes;
I would lead her through a garden of sly syncopations, slide
down slick mangrove leaves picking giant red and green flowers
called Calypso, Salsa, Mambo, away from music frozen
in shells of biker's meth, reefers soaking up stairwells;
we would flee felons, extortionists, shylocks, prostitutes,
pimps, bookies, all the coarse, pissed-off, hot-blooded
population sucking grace notes from breathable air;

we will disappear in a long conga line shaped like a Chinese
dragon, rhythm box head spitting fire from red ruby lips—
feel my woman's warm and winding hips transporting us
to celestial heights, tumbling through high notes together,
milky as stars exploding between her thighs.

THE LANGUAGE LOVER

> *All I know is what the world knows.*
> —Samuel Beckett

If you love the language, said my young professor
turning older, don't mess with mesostic text

In this blood-lit noir, disregard disjunction,
reification, visual & migratory malfunctions,

Take a lapse from the syntactic, deixes
of the elitist, write it as you see it, hear it, feel it,

For in the palimtext of life, it says that words
are fickle lovers, will leave you in the end.

THREE BLOCKS DOWN FROM HARRY'S BAR

After you leave the port captain's office
near the jetty
at the Grand Canal end of the Calle Valloresso
go to Harry's Bar next door
for a taste of peach juice called HARRY'S
WORLD-FAMOUS BELLINI, with *prosecco,* Venetian
champagne, dry and cold as a lover's lips
sensing indiscretions;—
toast the Scampi Man who wears a comical
monocle
big as an octopus eye; taste bay leaf
and rosemary sprig in the *zappa di pesce,*
then, mildly fortified

Stroll three blocks down from Harry's Bar,
far from the chilled-glass smiles of tourists
to a sailor's bar
where a 90-year-old woman dances for glasses
of local wine, words flow, dregs of the emotional
crush
flow freely
as from a broken tap on a big keg *of grappa.*

It is here
thirst for life goes on unguarded,
dignity and decorum purged in smokesweet air
as you climb up on the bar in front of the world
to dance with that old woman.

SEA CHILD

As the sea
feels tug of depth, sighs
of its shallows, the mother has her baby
in a *palapa* near the harbor.
Its father, a fisherman
searching for a catch on distant shores
senses a tremolent
in the current, jolt of hook, reddish
string of kelp transformed
to the umbilical of a miracle
caught in a Sargasso Sea of afterbirth
that brings the luxuriance
of new luck
equal now to the rich man
facing a school of tarpon.

OLD BUFFLECUPPER BEN

—Bend, Oregon

Everyone in our little lumber town
came down to the mill-pond
on that bright Spring morning
to pay last respects to Ol' Ben,
our state champion Bufflecupper,
dancer of logs, who, when called
by the river, sneaked by the night
nurse at the hospital like Banquo's
ghost to again be on line with the
box boom, pirouette on limbed &
rolling logs, leapt offstage
like Nijinsky through the curtains
of the Bolshoi, caught in a crush of
logs, smiling up at us in aqueous light,
as if he had found a sanctuary
of the spirit for us to remember him
in our town museum, his picture,
hobnailed boots, all to the shrill sound
of the unrelenting saws shaving
minutes from the hours until
the work whistle made its promise
of the night.

OLD MANUEL, CHRIST OF THE SEA

Out here, with the gilled & gutted,
fishing on the southwest chain of the Moros,
a vast blue plain, rising, falling, deeply
salted, more than one day of a ship's life,
the log of drowning, Old Manuel

Lies by the down-rigger on a mound of brailed
net, face color of dead yucca stalks near
his boyhood stream, the Rio Estrella,
River of Stars, back home; head tilted up
on a brinish kedge, eyes open . . .

"My God," says Cody, our young deckhand,
moral philosopher, on summer leave from UCLA,
"Manuel looks just like Christ—or maybe a 13th
Century Zen master from Dozen . . ."
we called Coast Guard, held hands, asked Jody

If he would close Old Manuel's eyes that appeared
to be challenging the sun.

THE PRESS CORPS OF XANADU

Think of thought's debris

Stored in vaults

Behind the retina's

Closed room of mirrors

The rose and lavender massage

Of political intrigue

By the press corps of Xanadu

Who hold cameras carelessly

As if always one more roll

Life can take if the eye

Can stand the answers

To all questions, false or true.

AN INTERVIEW WITH MR. BHUYANGASANA,
THE COBRA

With a slow, reaching hip-hop handshake,
Mr. Bhuyangasana, the cobra, uncoils from his mat,
thoracic spine, space between shoulder blades, unlimbers,

Says he's very pleased, grateful for the interview,
as I wait in the throes of immersion journalism
for his daughter, the interpreter, fluent in downtown Bantu

To arrive. In uneasy silence I feel the weight of his heavy-
lidded eyes, head swaying back and forth, long tongue
split, braided with sparkling stones, flicking a soft

Mist whose fluidity seems to tenderize the senses,
as if all in the room will soon be digested,
and the copy desk will wonder where I've gone.

WANDERLUST

> *A dry soul is best.*
> —Heraclitus

Down long green slopes
of the rain squalls, seabirds whip wind
with sodden feathers, boat stirs at mooring,
transient tides. We listen to the *chubasco's* hoarse
dark whisper, warning us, batten down
the hatches of our wanderlust,
reason for our restlessness
in the world's theatre
where storm and weather are but brief
intermissions
in searching for our lives.

GRANDFATHER, THE PEG AND BEAM MAN

As a small boy
I looked up at grandfather—
he was no two-by-four plank
trussing a wooden beam, but a giant
Oregon fir with no need of steel
nails, held together with tiny wooden pegs
of kindness, a sturdy structure
through all weather, peace and war—
as I grew older it seemed that grandfather
was a shelter for the spirit, pounded strength
of wooden pegs like European cathedrals,
Japanese pagodas, Amish barns—
and this is why grandfather's memory
still endures.

LISTENING TO CHARLIE

I'm listening to Charlie Parker's
Little Willie Leaps
skirling through woodsmoke
smelling
of coffee & creosote
from burning ties,
hoping my radio batteries
will hold
through Charlie's half-tone phrases,
sliding runs—
just what I need—
music with a little muscle
to help me climb back
on the train.

ODE TO A STAND-UP BASS

I listen

to the strict and somber music

polished in the wood.

Womanly, shapely, not cumbersome—

responding

to a little rub of rosin

on its strings, heartbeats

for its maestro, carried tenderly

over thresh-holds, jazz clubs, symphonic halls,

zipped tight in traveling suit,

paid passenger,

airports, subways, taxis—

most of all, to me, it seems, that during war

it grieves—

I hear in its deepest throbs

all the sorrows

of the world.

FAT LIVER'S HOT LICKS

Once I walked down Clay Street into Dai Fow, the Chinese
Big City in San Francisco, half a block below Du Pon Goi
or Grant Street to Fat Liver's shop (named from the French
foi gras). I found him snuggled in his drawstring parka
like a panda seeking warmth of snow. No heat in Fat Liver's
store—stacks of Mexican canned-abalone, aromatic smells
of Chinese sausage, roast pork, dried fish. Saxophones,
trumpets, snare drums, bass viols hung like dragon kites &
silk fans from the ceiling. Fat Liver was a godsend to poor
musicians. We'd pawn our instruments for a much lower rate
than the hock shop scalpers. "Oh yesssssss," Fat Liver
hissed joyfully, "The Slingerland drum kit kid." He said
this with a smile as wide as my Zildjian cymbal. To my surprise
he tore up my pawn ticket. "No charge, kid. Fat Liver must
confesss—I practicessss on your skinsss"—
It was then he put on an old Benny Goodman Quintet 48
featuring Gene Krupa on drums. He sat like a toy Buddha
on a soy sauce box, twirled sticks between thumb & fore-
finger with frisky aplomb, same driving beat, zokked rim-
shots with the master, stung the sock-cymbals, goaded
tom-toms into a furious rumble. Dusty displays danced with
stringy cobwebs in the window. People milled about & peered
inside. He ended the Krupa set by throwing a drumstick that
stuck in a pork loin. "You like Fat Liver's hot licks, kid? You cats
keep me working store day & night—so I wrote this for your
band to play." He tossed me his song, WOK AROUND THE
CLOCK BLUES, done with paintbrush on oiled paper. We did
our best for Fats—Berkeley was bewildered . . . , Modesto
mystified, but our gigs in Chinatown struck a vibrant chord.
His uncle put up money for three pressings, bought us a good
used bus & when the wheels turned our memories of Fat Liver's
hot licks rolled on & on & on.

THE MUSICIANS ARE PLAYING TONIGHT
   ## IN DREAMLAND

What about your music, man, what do you choose
to make your mark, leave behind?
You know the old saying, "Don't put your laundry in
for the first ten years"—but up here in Dreamland
I wished I had a few more labels—I liked Bill Basie's style,
living music of the instant, man, he'd get up from
his box, walk around, have a little taste with each sideman;
but Duke was the soul of creative discipline, a kind man
who kept key men playing at the Rainbow Room
with ascap & publishing money—took little Stray,
Billy Strayhorn under his wing—magnificent together—
I can still hear Ivory Anderson's voice late at night—
Duke's melody following chords—when restless I get out
Duke's *Mauve, Terribly Blue, Mood Indigo* . . .
Then I'll put little Jimmy Rushing on for those late-night
blues, nothing to do with Jimmy, he played alto, too,
but why did vocalists get drunk first? Must be backstage
and all that time . . . remember Johnny Hodges had RAB
marked on his sax parts because he looked like a rabbit . . .
one of my finest gigs was at the Newport Jazz Fes in '56 . . .
now if I had a few tracks of that, old friend, I'd say goodnight.

HIGHWAY 99

He had a rolling softness
in his talk, true Highway 99
truck-stop twang, a sound
Buck Owens brought
to Bakersfield in 1951;
resonates today in his Crystal
Palace, a new western country
style, high as the back of a
jazzed up cat, strings & horns
hav'n fun, get along;
and when I drive by broad fields
of ag & oil rigs, Buck's voice
still lingers in the music,
a great vitality, blue-collar men and
women, hard-earned dreamers,
aspirations, the real stewards
of the land.

CATCHING THE DREAM

. . . and then they came
when the risk to remain tight
in the bud was more painful
than the risk to blossom.
                    —Anais Nin

J.D. Salinger's young daughter kept her father's
famous book *Catcher In The Rye*
under her pillow so she could sleep at night.
Growing older she placed her memoirs,

The Dream Catcher, beside his where both books
would flit, swarm together like fireflies
in the dark. By morning light the airy pages returned
to their covers, nothing disturbed but pollen dust

On the wings of words.

A LETTER FROM MY FATHER TO HIS BROTHER BILL

To Bill:

Over seventy snows have melted since our Great Chief sent us out on the trail; each to accomplish a mission for Him. They were seventy cold, dark winters but we saw as many beautiful Indian summers. At times the trail became lost in the darkness of the night, but you and I could always depend on the little camp-fires of love which our mother kindled along the way. They still glow and always will.

On the thirty-first sun of the third moon and seventy-first year, deep shadows crowded the trail from view. There was only one way to look and that way was up.

I saw a silvery blue strip of heaven resting just on top of the tall dark trees and a very bright star was there. Somehow, Bill, I felt that you were very near and I wondered, had I faltered in my mission? You were called first by our Great Chief. Perhaps I grew tired, my feet lagged and while I rested you passed me by.

With wearied moccasins but resolute, I push the long trail behind. Perhaps a sun, a moon, or a few snows at most, I shall be called to the Great Council Chambers and you and I shall sit down together with our Great Chief and there shall be Peace Always.

Frank

Author's note: *My father, Frank Edward Dickson was raised on family ranch near the Nez Perce Indian Reservation, Colville, Washington. He and brother Bill's only childhood friends were Nez Perce, who taught them tracking, hunting, fishing. Chief Joseph, alive then, was famous for leading his entire tribe on over a 1,000 mile chase by the U.S. Calvary to near Canada, where he surrendered. Frank attended the Lake Chelan school, met my mother, Ada Chloe Dickson, who, at nine years of age, became Chief Joseph's trusted interpreter. He died before taking little Ada to the Washington D.C. Treaty Talks. My grandparents, Barnett and Dema Stillwell, were government appointed Principal/ Teacher and Reservation Nurse.*

CHIEF JOSEPH'S APPALLOOSA

From where the sun now stands . . .
—Chief Joseph, Nez Perce
Thunder Rolling In The Mountains
—Hin-Mah-Too-Yah-Lat-Ket

—to Mike C.

His horse, an Appalloosa, seeded in the high steppes
of Asia, appeared, withers to tail,
like a spotted faun blending with the forest,
white-rimmed eyes, gentle as a human's, a breed
admired, foals acquired from Spanish conquistadores
who swept up from the south in 1730, Mexico
to California, within reach of their beloved Willowa Valley
in eastern Oregon—
this valiant breed that outruns the U.S. Cavalry,
over a thousand miles to Bear Paw Mountain, Montana,
the Chief's surrender, 1877, within reach
of the Canadian border—
Chief Joseph, in beaded horn headdress, the Indian's Red
Napoleon, with stoic mien, dignity, surrenders—
accepts military orders of the tribe's
dissolution of their sacred Appalloosa (not wishing

such a nightmarish chase again)—
sold to ranchers, wheat farmers of the Northwest plains,
bred to draft & saddle horses, demeaned
to the depth of donkey unions—
one last gratuitous gesture, an Appalloosa left for
tribal culture, upon death of a warrior like Looking Glass,
this horse shall be saddled, without rider,
circle rows of teepees, carry the warrior's spirit
for both old & young to see, on, through
indignities, broken treaties, sunrise to dawn
when the spirit dismounts, forever moving on.

GRANDFATHER IN THE BASEMENT

Late at night grandfather's in the basement
bottling beer; he's like a leprechaun
dancing, singing, gamboling with the fungoids,
sampling his own art

Until a glassy grenade becomes overly yeasty,
explodes, awakening the house.
Grandmother comes down the stairs in her
carpet slippers and broom, wading through the carnage,
batting grandfather like a badminton bird
in a corner

Where he laughs and cries for getting caught
so near the threshold
of a cherished drunkenness, spitting broomstraw
from his mouth.

ON THE DAY REBA HAD HER
TATTOOS REMOVED

On the day Reba had her tattoos removed
Eagle flew from her fine human canvas

A pale green seahorse escaped its chain
On her ankle
A fish changing color under motel neon
In the rain
Melted into nothingness

Reba missed most of all her round little bear
Small as a fingertip, hibernating good-naturedly

Between folds of her most festive flesh
To be tickled, awakened by lovers
Who played with it joyously
Far into the early morning hours

As if the three of them were a family & she, Reba,
was the mother bear.

IT TAKES AN OLD WOMAN SCREAMING
VIETATO FUMARE!

It takes an old woman screaming
Vietato Fumare!
And beating
The hell
Out of you
With a broom

And believe me
You will stop smoking
In her parlor.

The world
Needs an old woman
Like that
With her broom
Of conviction

Strong enough
To stare down

The crocodile smile
Coiled somewhere
In the DNA
Of war.

BE PROUD YOU ARE AN INTELLECTUAL

When the old Russian poet visiting our school
told us about Stalin, long Siberian nights
and fellow prisoners leaching salt
from the guards' beating canes
for their rations of frozen potatoes
we stopped badgering our parents
for more all-day burritos and double-orders of fries
washed down with perplexing decisions
between coke, pepsi, mountain dew and doctor pepper.
He told us to go to the library
because they are all over our great country,
warm in winter, cool in summer,
librarians wearing pretty dresses—
spend time there, he said, learn something
interesting to you as an individual,
be like I am, he said, stand up for things
you believe in, be proud you are an intellectual.

I WRITE HER NAME ON RICE PAPER

I write her name on rice paper; swallow her down
with the wine;—
    remembering the north shore of Santa Cruz Island
called *Cuevas Pintado* by Cabrillo
    in 1542;—
we were shy together, recently met, assured the Greek's
    Oceanus
meant the beginning of all things,
    floating through the grand arch of a strange new world,
limestone walls salted white
    in darkness of greens & yellow shimmerings, pulse
of our love like fish
    flashing silver patterns on the basalt floor,
in the seawomb riding swells, passing by
    three exiting waves, four, then five
until the tourist boat nudges our bow in torchlight
    with cries of the old world
to be rinsed from our ears by the seabirds
    waiting for us, outside.

SOMEWHERE IN THE MUSIC AND THE DANCING

—to Kev C.

Hitching on the Pan-American highway beyond Lima,
villages with bark-less dogs drugged on sun, sweet smell of
decaying burros sprinkled with mounds of windblown
sand without centerline but for the eyes' split vision,
clouds clinging like un-licked stamps to blue envelope of
sky addressed to all life below in lazy scrawl of buzzards,
black nights with stars like spy-holes in a giant cell door.
No train sounds to pierce the air, hoarse harsh whistles
when riding the container car south to Memphis, Texas
party music of Ciudad Juarez across from El Paso, no sad
border town tone of the *Maquilladores los Dondillas* where
she would dance and he would play guitar, music pressed
against pale distance until bones of compression cry out
for home; her moist young face reddening under white
bean pesto, wearing a beaded dancing dress over jeans and
boots so it will not wrinkle, a bra string trailing from her
small cane suitcase with the UCLA sticker, his guitar
strung down back like a field worker's child, the blue
tattooed snake with red eyes coiling down arm where his
fret hand had touched, stirred her softness, more ravishing
than the flesh of music, delirious dialogue of their love:
*Your guitar tells me what's in your heart, Your dancing is the
breath of love;* both remembering their last 3-peso bath,
waiting turns behind a burlap curtain as old women under
punched oil drums dribbling orange water show flashes of
pubis like small triangular patches of vulcanized rubber,
grandchildren laughing, clinging to legs, old men sipping
aguardiente between siesta snoring. With warm water
cooling her body she thinks of orange monkey flowers,
Monterey pines, he thinks of a cold Atlantic off Jersey's
shore; both dread the hitching, separations, oil truckers
stopping, motioning for the girl. He marvels at the way
she steels herself, staring straight ahead in the cab without
waving goodbye as he sits on his bedroll picking chords,

face without emotion, that he'll get a ride by and by, share driving, fix a tire, help with loading, unloading; both know that nothing in this world will keep them from meeting at the next truck-stop, and each must go alone in one's skin while heart and mind belong to the other, that they'll meet somewhere in the music and the dancing later on.

IDENTITY BY THE NUMBERS

To others, my identity may be perplexing,
but not to me, to mend, I blend,
I can be Alsatian, Euratian, a fake albino
with speckled skin, suffer no cultural
miscalculations, or boring monologue with
pain, everyone who is living life struggles
with its design, desires a more subtle
architecture of the spirit, a risky ride to
heritage & pride, be unafraid, let your hours
stir blood of colors, learn to laugh a little
more each day.

SEARCHING FOR SWANIE'S BOAT

The sun's a brazen gong struck over Delta waters.
Engine's 2/4 throb echoes in the inlets. On the way

To Windmill Cove for Taco Tuesday, toast the day
at the Sawlty Dog at Herman & Helens,

Searching for Swanie's boat, query friendly river-rats,
follow a slow clamshell dredge down Railroad Cut

Between The Old and Middle Rivers, prow cutting
through sawgrass green as a sea of dollar bills

Tourists thumbtack on Al-The-Wop's ceiling
at the early Chinese city of Locke. At night lights

On water become flitting fireflies of red and green,
listening to live music from fire-lit beaches, still

Searching for E.D. 'Swanie' Swanson's boat, a nostalgic
mission in memory of his north Hollywood Swanson

Agency where many a novel gave life to film, my first
agent I still remember fondly, following clues along

The San Joaquin for his '57 Chris-Craft classic
with the bewitching name, KWITCHURBELYAKIN,

A feeling I would take to heart because that's the way
he'd want it, but memories of Swanie's kindness

Would not fade away, sail on and on and on . . .

HARD STREETS WITH GRIEF'S SOFT EDGES

I'm one of many poets
who have seen hard streets with grief's soft edges,
kilometers from constitutional guarantees,
foreign soil far from city bus stops, old palms brittle with age,
bars over windows, steel-mesh trash bins whiskered
with rust, fierce alley dogs sniffing for *dineros,*
mangy, territorial . . .

Shhhhh! Quiet. Listen for the rare sound of an air conditioner,
a place without night sweat, mosquitoes,
prepared, once again, to sleep on a floor—perhaps luck
of an old man and his woman, tenderness and drunkenness
hold hands in the dark, amnesty of food, work—*AY Dios*—
as if all inwardness has been rehearsed on the stage
of life before . . .

Drowsing in old vegetable oil odors, *arrez con polla,*
ropa viejo, the spicy chicken smell, how a full warm belly
can deceive the mind for a moment, the animal inside
will cease its clawing, absolve all shame in silent prayer,
believe once again in the young lovers, kissing
away each other's tears in the next room, whispering,
in a strange language, that the world may be

Wounded, but we'll all go on together, and the stranger
slept until roosters cracked the dawn.

WOMEN'S VOICES

I like to listen
to women's voices,
a casual listening post
without intrusion,
garage sales, farmers'
markets, shared
communication centers,
and, as some have said, a nest
of spiders spinning webs
of gossip, nothing could be
farther from the truth,
drifts of airy laughter, breezy
as clean sheets on a morning
clothesline, swept by winds
of trust & love, voices
joined at town meetings,
a mother's hard reality whose
timelines are fusing, miracle
of birthing, where no man
has been before. I want women's
honesty to be national, enduring,
Senators, Congresswomen,
I'd cast my vote for president,
one just like my mother,
her smile of hope, world at peace,
the whole nation rocking in her arms.

THE INVITATION

She wore the sun

As a white lace collar,

A queenliness

Gracing

Her abode, soft

Resonance of voice

Asking me in,

Feel comfortable, she said,

See if your soul

Feels at home, if so,

Your room is ready,

And the poetry

Can begin.

A DAY IN THE NIGHT OF THE IGUANA

I lie awake by the deserted set by the sea,
my head on the two-tank dive gear,
listening to rain press-roll on the roof
of corrugated tin, date palm frond
scratching a maraca beat on the *palapa's*
window, sea shimmers fitfully, teases
the chubasco out of its cave, half-dreaming
I'm a Perseus south of the border,
saving Andromeda from the sea monster,
her tears of gratitude drying on someone else's
shoulder, sea-salt sheen of flesh rewarding
another extra, head on arm, breathing deeply,
as if sleep is imperative, forming sea
crystals of her beauty no film has yet captured
in the opening night of dreams.

HOPE IS THE THING WITH FEATHERS

before going to the library to get warm,
become steam-heated by the librarian's woolen
skirts he didn't know Keats from Yeats,
Creon's son from Laertes' father—
invited seven times now by the librarian
for tea in her flat above the used-book store
he brought her day-old flowers from the alley
behind the Chinese funeral parlor & a package
of seeds for her little parakeet
that seemed to symbolize a line of Emily Dickinson:
"Hope is the thing with feathers."

ANTOJITOS

She wears
her collection
of *antojitos,*
little whims of finery,
dazzlers
    drenched
with humor, serenity,
as if the sun pinned tiny invitations
on her body for the boy,
now a young man, to remember.

THE SAN FRANCISCO PIT BAND BLUES

back when six-a-day vaudeville was alive
& frisky & the drummer's rimshot tagged
the dancer's body at the apex of her thrust
the albino piano player smoked the ivories
with both hands, keys all nicotined
with yellow & stained with gin
the pit band shared a room in a fleabag
across from the rialto & after the gig
monsoon the bass player goes down to the
st. francis with his bass he calls billy,
so monsoon & billy prowl the hotel party
rooms set up for the sales conventions,
loads billy's plaid-striped carrying case
with knockwurst, pickles & good italian
bread, tucks in a brew or two, goes back
to our room with all this tasty larder &
we give turk a call—turk murphy was a
big-time musician who lived to play his horn,
so turk mutes his trombone with a red-rubber
plunger & the drummer used hair brushes
on the sports page of the chronicle & clovis
our cute little vocal takes turk's socks off
to make us some hard-boiled eggs she held
under the hot water-tap until they were done
& monsoon breaks out the brew we spike with
kesslers until we all feel half-snoggered
& mellow & clovis called some dancers from a
chinese chorus line & the music whispered
sort of private, low-down & cozy, even fooled
the hotel dick until four-thirty in the morning
& by that time we had most of what life had
to offer.

ON THE BUS TO MAZATLAN

I catch
a second class bus
to Mazatlan
filled with standers
and the usual two drivers
in case
one goes loco.
I pass them a note
in Spanish,
"I am Ramondo,
the gringo *escribér*.
If you need
another spare driver,
please
let me know."
When the driver
reads the word *escribér*
he smiles, nodding *Si*
in the rear-view mirror.

DRINKING ROOT LIQUOR, SPITTING
LIKE A LLAMA

Somewhere between life's strandings
and groundings
I remember the old blind man of Michoacán
and three beautiful daughters
he kept prisoners in an old Spanish colonial
(except for the celebration
called the *Cry of Dolores*)

Children gave him a crushed armadillo
on a stick fresh from the highway;
he thought the gift was a suckling pig
until he picked through its shattered armor;
cursed the *niños* with considerable color
as the circle of small faces drew back
like a shade from an intolerable sun . . .

I remember a truckload of young men serenading
his daughters who waved bits of provocative clothing
from a broomstick in an upper window
as a sign of surrender; inspired the choir a capella
to sing on and on and on . . .

The old blind man of Michoacán sat guarding
the doorway, listening to love songs
in his scarred *bandelero,* tapping time
with a big black revolver he had from the wars
of Pancho Villa; drinking root liquor,
spitting like a llama,
rocking the bloody armadillo in his arms
like a newborn baby

Until the flatbed of serenaders pulled out
at dawn, still singing, swearing to again
meet his daughters, saving pesos for candles,
and by the time of *The Cry of Dolores*
praying the old man would be gone.

CREDO

Not all poetry is the prosaic entrance,
signification and revelatory endings.
Life isn't that well packaged, except,
perhaps, the *entrado* (entrance)
championed by Octavio Paz in Mexico
City before his death. Narrative poetry,
in particular, is crafted from sequence
and consequence, a story line every time,
reticulation of diversity, humanity, love
of language. I find today's young poets
spice it with inventiveness, intriguing
personas, candid compression,, anything
that works, double associations, triple
internal rhythms, sound of line endings,
aesthetic complexities, supple movement,
because, after all, we live in a changing
new world of ideas and feelings, it takes a
poetry to match.

ODE TO AN IMPUDENT FLEA

High above me I watch the lovers
Perform like brave aerialists
Without a net; their kisses swinging on silken
Strings of air,
As I, a petulant flea, burrow deeper into the sweet
Musk of her bramble, taking, once again,
Her hand from his stubbled cheek
To scratch away my impudence.

THE WOMAN OF YOKOHAMA

made lamps of mulberry bark, *wooshi* paper,
      higo from bamboo; her eyes
filled with surprise
      as someone sees the ocean
for the first time, fires
      in the irises
reflecting garnets, lapis, amethyst,
      cooled by sight
of surf at night
      unrolling long white curls
of silk chiffon.

      When her fingers moved
under low and mellow light
      no one could convince me
she was blind.

AT THE HARBOR LIGHTS BALLROOM

Lights from the oil rigs off Santa Barbara
slip & slide
across the sea's glassy ballroom floor,
dip like tango dancers
in dark corners
to scritchy music from Asia

Brightening wheelhouse windows
as if reflecting time
in revolving balls of ceiling lights
of old ten-cents-a-dance palaces

Where lonely men, vowing to swim or drown,
once plunged into perfumed waves
of flesh, dance tickets trailing
over her shoulders
like kelp to shorerock

Or more precisely
in this harbor light, cut flowers
swirling in flotsam drift
from the funeral boat

Knowing each flower once blazed
with a color of its own.

1959: THE YEAR BILLIE HOLIDAY DIED

I liked the raw silk of Billie's voice, her husky
inner-tones that told you she had been every place
you have gone & will be going because at thirteen
she had experienced the forces of hell. I thought
of needle tracks police found on Billie like blue
spider webs spread across dark moist skin, her
ticket from private to public hospital, chained to
her bed, stash of heroin money, a few fifty-dollar
bills taped to her body in a place her manager's
thieving fingers couldn't feel. In my writer's muse
I produced a sympathetic character called Martin,
a young black orderly who read Yannis Ritsos, Octavio
Paz & Lorca paperbacks, who also memorized Billie's
troubled bio when reading *The Grey Lady* on the metro.
Martin knew Billie was a granddaughter to a slave, took
her father's name, a musician who abandoned her mother
when Billie was two; arrested with her mother for pros-
titution in 1928, a world of clients like giant fork-
lifts of brutality who could pick up & slam down the
human merchandise; her mother dead at forty-four, a
delirious desecration of body & soul by drugs & alcohol;
Billie stepping over suicides like a dancer at the Bolshoi;
1928, the year Billie tried her luck in Harlem, no, she
didn't dance, but I can sing, sang "Travelin', Travelin'
All Alone," not a dry eye in the house, discovered by John
Hammond, Count Basie, Benny Goodman & Artie Shaw in
1933; toured south in first black/white band, bitter tension,
racists called her that nigger whore who sang the old
protest song, "Strange Fruit;" married Sonny Monroe,
still a druggie, learned bass line of pure heartbreak,

movie, *Symphony In Black*, 1947, another heroin bust,
received a year & a day, denied a cabaret license,
moved to Paris, accepted as jazz royalty; hospital death scene
with young black orderly called Martin weeping bitterly.
He's fingering the tag on her toe as if he could change
the name & Billie could go on singing.

WHEN DIAMOND TEETH MARY SINGS
THE BLUES

Old Mary, who doesn't drink, smoke, dip or
chew
is back on a little down-South stage; she says,
before every performance

I don't want to, but I've got to sing the blues.

Foil gum wrappers replaced the diamonds long ago
to pay the lady's way;—
sparkled, then, in the fine blue smoke of measured
truths
of which she had never cut a side.

One can count on a moment in the set
when both soft-drinkers & hard-drinkers
give respectful silence

I know this ain't no church, she says

as she spreads her hands like dark wings
of a wounded bird
released from the earth in song.

SAILOR SONG

We leave with a norther blowing, a claw to weather,
house holes leaking the sea's tears,
smell of the small wild boar speared for stew,
sweet tea for washing down the edible bird's nests,
scent of sandalwood and camphor sloshing
in the scuppers—
taking comfort in our great white wings, the solid
heavy plodding of the ketch, a modified
fin keel underbody with a skeg hung rudder
that has pointed true as a compass needle to secret
places of the world.
No GPS, global positioning system, to check each
hour, nor aimless drift of life making love
to a winch, rattle of rigging on nasty seas that
flatten into the Atlantic chop, coastal
Panama, northern Caribbean, great cruising grounds
of Honduras, Guatemala, Belize, six-hundred miles
across the Gulf of Mexico, take a tot, a thimble
of Scotch to the chart's inaccuracies.

Hurricane holes, clear weather windows, yachts
moored to the quay wall at Horta in the Azores,
on to Ireland, Fastnet Light, Emerald
Isle to Cork . . .

Singapore to Hawaii via Rabaul and Canton Island,
weaving Turks Head knots in 20-degree rolls,
crew auditioning for parts in Billy Budd
dragging the anchor of our anguish in a hurricane,
boat breaking, sinking, no one left in the world
but silent figures in Kuna *molas* walking toward us
through the surf, arms outstretched, welcoming us
to their shores.

OVER THE FAR HORIZON

We must humor the crazy old woman in charge
of the winds, knotting, knitting,
unspooling the sea. She likes to hear *guitérons,*
didjeridus, seashells blown like mouth-harps
of the deep, kettlepan drums from the galley.
We must not take notice of ragged skirt, scale
of winds sung in hollow voice, torn straw hat
woven with rain clouds and seabirds, legs
that need shaving. We must compliment her frizzed
hair-do tied in pinwheels of line squalls,
lightening bolts, ignore lipsticked gash of mouth
puckered for wicked kisses, toast her in the wheel-
house with island rum and coffee. We must humor
the widow of Odysseus, sister of wind demons, the
Norse god Thor, Fujin of Japan, Ehecatl, the Aztec
dancing monkey god, Hung Kong, birdlike god of the
winds of Taiwan and Raijin, spirit of thunder
on his ring of drums. We must help pack her suitcase,
tattered silks spilling blackness, wave her off
before the barometer reaches twenty-eight inches,
row her to the bus for Galveston, bring down hatches
on her rank perfume, pray the feathery dark smudge
on skyline is but oily smoke-rings from a hobo freighter,
not her complimentary tornado; we are changing course
for a secure salvation, rising, falling, somewhere
over the far horizon.

THE NAVIGATOR

The crew thinks he is talking to seabirds.
Salt water blisters break like scuttling crabs
Across his body. He sits forward
Reading water as if the sea were an old testament
Of swells and sliding currents.
At night he sits alone staring at the star, Polaris,
Remembering his father's lessons, each star
A coral shell
Pushed with pointed stick across the beach's
Sandy heavens
Toward a half-submerged coconut, their voyage's
Destination; chanting all the while
To the sea gods
To supplement his navigation.

TETAUTUS

—to Kev C.

Across the five-mile lagoon to Tetautus
speed boats strike light like aluminum spears
flung at the sun . . .
she stands in her floral dress in the pink & yellow
plumosa trees
beside her white-haired father in flour-sack shorts.
He helps with new varnish, waxes the hull;
she cultivates a secret breadfruit of the spirit,
tends chickens, herds pigs
down the crushed coral pathways of the motu,
one of hundreds scattered like bright industrial
shells
across the atolls.

When she walks into their cinder-block house
to face me
the wind drops to calm . . .

Before the storm season when it is time to leave
she weaves pandanus mats for the cabin floor.
Her father presents a frond-lined box
of drinking nuts, saying

the flying fish must come down & wet
his wings
or it will never fly again . . .

They go with me as I pay the $20 per-person
exit fee
to the sweatless consul
buttoned tight in white serge drill: one dollar
for the agricultural agent
(he sprayed the boat for copra bugs) & $1.75 per day
for anchoring in the lagoon.

Although English is a second language in French
Oceania
we never spoke of love—
but when she places the flower crown upon my head
& touches my hair
the old man smiles his gentle smile & wind freshens
heavy harbor chop
as I untie the boom-vang's choke upon the sails,
follow an inter-island copra boat through tricky
coral shelf
before opening his gift to toast the sunset
& my island hosts, surprised to find in the drinking pod
a $20 bill;
perhaps my pardon, as an early convict of Tongareva
was once released from Paradise
to the open gates of sea.

LONG AFTER THE BOATS HAVE GONE

As night conceives the sea-sounds in silence,
And out of their droning sibilance makes a
serenade.

—Wallace Stevens

She comes to him
    when the sea is soundless as a tired whale
drifting on silent flukes; krill rising
    from cold depths
through pale clouds of copepods; faint clicking
    of dolphins
bellies fat with squid, riding rollers into shore.

The only sound,
    low-frequency baritone of the bottom trawler's
diesel screw
    plowing on as darkness falls, fishermen's dreams
become drift creatures
    like larvae shrimp who hide from light
of day, rise

For food of night,
    swirling veils of luminescence
glowing
    in glassy spicules of waves
long after the boats have gone.

GUS, CHEF DU MONDE

We cruise past giant slabs of hotel light
shredding sea's darkness, stabbing surfline
until dying in fitful shadows. We sail by
seaside palaces employing imported chefs, presenting
the world's most expensive menus.

Our chef Gus laughs and sings, flings splashes
of ouzo that flame to the color of his
bloodshot eyes, prepares a multisplendored
Aegean spread off Miami, spicy callabo soup
he learned from the Aussies, a seafood salad

Seasoned with habanera peppers, fillets a red
rockcod fresh from our hook, dominates his small
galley with sharp eyes of a shoebill stork,
admonishes his parrot, Piedra, for sly picking
at delicacies like a tern stealing fish from

A brown pelican's pouch. Gus's tab is never
exorbitant a few satisfied belches, kudos fit
for the greatest of Greeks—an extra hour or two
of shore leave most crucial to love's survival—
for Gus is a ladies' man who likes to scan the menu.

THE TOW TO MAZATLAN

> —for Wolfgang, Beth, Oregon Bob,
> Delta Dave, Fast Jack, Carquinez Dick,
> Louie & Jan

The old singlehanding Swede called Sven
looks like a cross between a rooster fish
and a thresher shark
in his eelskin suspenders & canvas shorts.
Sven sits in his leaking gaff-rigged cutter
on the swelling salt-buffed Sea of Cortez
rising and falling like a tropic bird off
the East Cape of Baja, 45 miles from Jose del
Cabo, 65 miles from La Paz (he wrote this down
on a green sea turtle shell for insurance purposes)
as we give old Sven an extra pump and a four-hour
tow to Mazatlan.

We hear Sven's strong voice over shrieking caw
of seabirds, old eyes round as blue aggies
young boys shoot in a ring of the sun;
—he speaks of fish in a way that makes us forget
the marlin count at Cabo San Lucas;
between stories he rubs his old body to a rubicious
glow with a seaweed called Turkish Towel;
tosses fishheads to the gray-headed nobbies,
laughing as they fight off black and white terns.
"I've fished the remote shores of Golfo Dolce
near the Panamanian border, caught amberjack
and dog-toothed snapper, sailed the rivers of Costa
Rica—the Tortugero—Parismina, in sight of the
Caribbean . . ."
On and on, over the diesel's throaty throb,
Sven's pig-iron stubbornness on his favorite subject—
"I've heard cries from the gutted heart
of fish—the natives' cry of *sabalo!* for leaping
jungle river tarpon; hell, I traded my Howler monkey

& a yellow toucan for a night of love
in a village in low-lying mangrove-cays in the Turneffe
Islands of Belize" (do we hear him right—is he
switching from fish to love?)
"I dream of mermaids on long voyage
swim with them in their spangled
nakedness, you should see us together, a lyric
piscine movement under tons of water light,
a prelude to the time I need ashore—my body
lusts for the female species, lads, like a bonefish
in frenzy of a feeding cycle; floundering
in sinful waters, an excursion—there—
in her narrow room on an armoire above the bed—
a tall cardboard figure of Christ (blood-red enamel
wounds trailing down, congealing on the surface
like fishblood in a cuddy) precisely then
I kicked out in sheer exultancy of the moment,
climaxing like a sailfish leaping in the body's
sun until Christus comes tumbling down upon
our forms as if to monitor our liaison;
the well-seasoned prostitute begging marriage,
when, nearing the shores of spiritual conversion, I
over-tip for votive candles . . ."
Sven's voice over strong winds as choppy waters
sounds like fluttering canvas on the halyards.
He tells of coral-encrusted sea mounds, blotched
flats, snorkeling up on snooks; taste for permit, jacks,
barracuda, snappers, groupers;
love of village women, high trees, rain forests, collection of
calypso, reggae records, bullfishing
on Guanacante in Flamingo Bay, Cabot Island, Quepos,
near San Jose where schools of blue marlin congregate
in July, August and September.
"Why haven't you asked me about my greatest fish?"—
without a pause for breath—"It was a great blue
marlin like your own Ernesto Hemingway's *The Old Man
and the Sea*—caught on a flying fish sewed on a
bone hook taught to me by the Indians—
I was trolling in the blue's spawning cycle—

she was stippled in soft pewter light showing finery
of her cobalt body—I knew she was female—surfing
with six small male fish sporting like kids at your
Redondo Beach in California, surging down the sigh
of wave, spurred, of course, by nature's promise—
why you and I go to sea, lured by tropic
transiency—why fish follow below our water-lines
peering up at us through salt-licked eyes
of water at our pitiful little journeys . . .
I cut the line, of course, set free out there
in specks and sparks of grayish-white bathing
in the dull red ball of sun."
Sven seems to echo the hissing sigh of his bow
cleaving water bluer than Mexican tile found
in the fountain plazas of Guadalajara.
Our eyes burn as we search for the dark loom
of Mazatlan.
"It is best out here," shouts Sven, as if sensing
our impatience with his stories, mouth moving
through salt-white beard with each word
pushed out against the new warm land wind,
sun glinting off his polished teak skin like an
ancient black-boned pyrate relishing our obedience
to his songs.
"Out here—crystal clean," Sven's voice intones,
"free from sandbars, mudflats, big flies, hungry
peros—far from the tiresome twirling on your
hook, oily languidness of harbor smells—severed
heads of rotten mangoes sprinkled with coffee grounds,
condoms, like miniature half-swamped canoes
tossed out by the gringo yachties . . .
Yachties!" (Sven shouts with disgust) "are called
papalangis on Tongatapu in the southernmost part
of the Kingdom of Tonga—ruled by one King and
thirty-three Nobles of the Realm . . . I remember
a thatched *fales,* a house, sheltered deep in the
root-tangled Burau trees—this *fales* reserved
at three-dollars each for a dancing party,
something this old Swede loves to watch and do

for dancing is but a different form of sailing—
recruitment for my social life—something those
filled with life can identify . . . milling outside were
pigs, dogs, cats, goats, horses & fold-up bicycles;
hall decorated with tree branches and plumeria
leaves for the crazy papalangis. We revelers ate
roast pig, marinated raw fish, root crops and greens
with our fingers. A band of drums, ukuleles & one
steel guitar stirred frangipani sweetness
of the air. After my long sea journey I was parched
for the Dance of Love; fell in the deeps of desire
for the featured dancing girl who danced the *Tamure*
under soft light of kerosene lamps, arms beckoning
singlehanding Swede from Stockholm, a luring
motion as if spun filaments of flesh and shadow,
stunned by her body's artful invitation whispering
in the half-darkness of her grass skirt;—
it surely wasn't the bottle of Aquavit I saved
for such occasions that summoned sexual tremors
in my blood, but the thrumming *thump thump thump*
of her hand beating time on her belly, the tight-
skinned instrument stunning senses, driving me
out on the dance floor, to do my version of the *Tamure,*
in doing so, congratulate her and break the spell.
To my astonishment I had irritated the natives
(I think they were her brothers) who thought I had
demeaned a sacred art, and so initiating a fresh
departure, as we sailors say; gift of my binoculars
to Customs in return for clearance & thoughts of
her still aching in me, loins awash in the bilge
of guilt and Aquavit, watching coconut fringe
of the island become the dark lashes of the dancing
girl until fading from the atoll, with nothing ahead
but the pounding heart of sea."

Gulls swoop down severing old Sven's monologue,
beady black eyes on swivelstick necks,
swarming like a disinherited people, a mob
without formation

181

scattering ferocious hunger, scrambling horn-toed
on his fantail for the bucket of fish-scraps.
We wonder why he incites, feeds this beating
feather-mop of frenzy, beaks that had
surely violated their own family nests, dripping
yellow yolks of brothers and sisters . . .
"It's true!", Sven shouts, as if in answer—"their
hunger is honest—in the open—yet they represent
scum society of the sea, so why should I go ashore
to see what they do well? Over there the world
lives in an ecru-colored shell fragile to the sound
of guns. My tender incubated ears
seek shelter from man's cunning carnage; I have
storm'sl rigged long before birthing squalls
curse the mother, whore of wars, and the long vanished
bastard father. Landlubbers should ask the question:
what's a politician without his or her constituency?"

We take Sven to a Mazatlan bar refusing
to take our money (honoring anniversary date
of the death of Hemingway); Papa's picture,
signed, hangs over backbar by an oil painting
of *Leda and the Swan*—Ernesto stands by a great
blue marlin . . .
we get the old man fed (had we heard him bargain for a
woman's bed?); help patch his old
double-ender, spent another week listening
to his stories, trying to trip him up to no avail
at twice-told tales, his old sun-speckled hands
moving like Von Karajan's
directing vicissitudes of the seven seas,
skin of mottled blue stretching like a nautical map
with tales of ten-thousand atolls
between the Indian subcontinent, Arabian peninsula,
Africa, bold adventures on a lateen-sailed dhow
in the Maldives . . .

We wave farewell from the quay as Sven grins
with teeth of bronze swordfish darts

182

made for him by a Chinese dentist in Macao
(we now know why Sven was known locally as *El Rey
de los Feos,* King of the Ugly)
—boyishly, he touches a rigging kit he keeps
in a cowhide sheath
like a gunslinger stalking Neptune; watch him
kiss an ardent woman with three daughters
who present Sven with a small sun parasol fringed
with either old-fashioned underwear or Spanish
shawl; see him shove off with his saltiest salute,
beating on a biscuit-tin with a big wooden
galley spoon, ripple of fish behind his wake,
white blanket of birds to keep him company,
boat half-swallowed by the fiery rim of sea
until Sven's sails are just a scratch of light
silvery as fish-scales
scattered on the horizon of his restlessness
as we return to our long-necked Dos Equis,
savored now with the taste of loss.

EZRA POUND AND THE RASTAFARIANS

I am sitting on my snaredrum case.
Rastafarians are passing a big joint around.
We talk openly with quiet spirit
about the tinder box called race. Old sayings
make the rounds: "Hatred destroys the one
who hates"; "'Myth is gossip growing old'
Ezra Pound," says one dragging deep;
"Debate is good for the constitution," says
another, "statecraft or gentry"; "Underneath
layers of our art is the iconic testing
of our beliefs," says another, his words
have a mellow flavor; "Yes, mon, be it Tel
Aviv or Buenos Aires, the sacrifices
swoon to sleep." At last its my turn to take
the doobie, "'The Negro is America's metaphor,'
Richard Wright." I wish I had said that,
my friends, but alas, I'm white.

CHANO: SUBTLETIES OF THE BEAT

I watched dancers
at the old El Floradito Restaurant
in Los Angeles
twine like anacondas
in leafy jungle trees, writhing
to Afro-Cuban Latin rhythms
in colored silks of fragrant smoke
as Chano, the bearded Cuban drummer
mesmerized dancers with his congas,
knowing that love alone
will awaken them, uncoil their dreams,
release them from dexterous
subtleties,
the crushing power of his beat.

UNDER THE WINE PALMS

Bird dancing season. Lingering scent of nutmeg
over water. What is more voluptuous than Time

Sharing a narrow beach under the wine palms,
head on pillows of sand shaped like a woman's breasts?

In the dream I am Columbus at the mouth of the Rio Belem,
ship too large for rig and burthen, transported

By native sloop, small trading trunk filled to brim
with silver reals, gold pieces, Excelentes

Of Ferdinand and Isabella—and then—miracle of
miracles before waking—a female guide beside—

And when I whisper in her ear it goes straight through
to God on the other side. He appears to listen,

Smiles, shakes his head, waves a cautioning finger,
that I'm dallying with the Mother Superior,

Better sail on to Portland, Oregon, where I belong.

COCONUT MILK & ISLAND RUM

He's awakened by that old drummer rain
press-rolling on a tin roof,
a zip-zap rhythm like crazy musicians
playing medieval bagpipes, conch shells,
congas & mbiras. He's fiddling with a long
cumbersome word his pain had invented, something
to explain this dreary morning: *alcomelancholic*
he writes in the sand
to be brushed away by a sly spider monkey
when he turns to his first drink of the day,
coconut milk & island rum.

THE TRADER

He went down to the used parts house of the body
to trade his fibula for a tibia
& when the parts man wasn't looking
he'd fondle old bones of burlesque queens,
rub sleek shanks of ballroom dancers,
touch bony hands of concert pianists whirling
dust;—
he liked most of all to feel the pale patina
of an old skull & its emanations—
a strange warmth imparting wisdom & for this
fine bone vessel
with its logbook of a trillion voyages,
he would trade it all.

THE SOUND OF SEÑOR POCAROO'S
MULTICULTURAL BAND

In the nightlit pharmacopoeia of my jazz addict's
brain
I fly like a Monarch butterfly from southern California
to Mexico City
to hear Señor Pocaroo' s multicultural sound.
He wears a short white ponytail harnessed
by a rubber band, brocalette eyebrows dyed rust-red
sagging like old sofas over his eyes.
He plays an African *mbira,* thumb piano with a bandaged
thumb. His brother-in-law, Koko Rios, plays a Japanese
samisen with a banjo-like sound; his uncle Rico Redfern
plays a Korean *miguk piri,* a double-reed woodwind
backed up
by a ferocious young drummer with no name
banging on a Japanese *daiko* two-headed drum.
A thin black man, Calvin from Shreveport, Louisiana,
blows the blues on a Chinese mouth organ
called the *sheng.* All coalesce into a thrashing
pricking sound with icepick jabs of drum and cymbals.
The second tier carries soul of the band's book,
memorized, lying mute in tissue, sealed in the foundry
of flesh. The band invited, with exception of a few past
years
to the rhumba competition in Matanzas, the Cuban port city
where they have learned the Mantanzan purification
chants
adding to their repertoire of the Yoruban possessive
dances. The wooden drum boxes called *cajones*
are booming—the *lyessa,* set of three handheld drums,
one waist high, spitting firedrops of jungle rhythms.
A *nganga* magic pot is stirred with hand-stroked
murmurings.

At last, fevers unabated, we music lovers
push forward

as Señor Pocaroo presents his starshell of the
evening, a Miss Lotus Leotardo, curve some instrumentalist
from Milan
who begins her solo lying on her back on a woven
Peruvian rug. One can hear, at first, a faint tracery
of sound, bracelets brushing skin like muted
castanets. "A physical spirituality," explains Señor
Pocoroo, "authentically recorded, get your set
in compact discs or cassettes—"

I hear a throbbing, rising and insistent, an exultant
energy
shimmering in the music of her ankle bells. My God,
with intense concentration, Miss Leotardo is fondling
her instrument, not unlike a feathersoft stroking on
a Javanese *gamelon,* pleasuring herself!
Long before her ninth curtain call I placed my order
with Señor Pocaroo, ears unappeased and burning
for the sound.

PACA AND THE SALMON RUN

The part-time deckhand wears sneakers
bleached white from carwash soap;
sea is flat gray with a queasy rise
of his hangover, light northwest winds
mottle waves like tomcat fur . . .

Boat meets the swells doggedly
as last night's barmaid
cutting off his drinks; she, too,
was efficiently cheerful
in her wide chines & small keel

As they pass through the Golden Gate,
roam outside from Pescadero to Double Point
for market-size salmon, their broad silver
sides brightening mist rising from the water

Downriggers set, lines snapping from clips
like a waitress snatching orders
from a chef's wheel; skirting shallows
off Martin's Beach, down the southside
outside the North buoy

Easing through schools of krill & anchovy,
salmons' feeding ground, boxing limits
of splitters & slugs, lunkers for freezers
commanded by fishermen's wives . . .

It's out about here that Little Paca, Pacalengua
from Manila, goes crazy, laughing into the wind,
wielding his fishknife like a pool shark pointing
with his cue

where our body parts, filleted with flashing speed
would go. "Heyyyy, Paca—easy man" soothes

the skipper but Paca crouches at the fantail,
body wire-tight, head curled down like a single
hook set-up, light froth of salt-white spit
drools down his chin

as gulls wheel away from his shrill mad music,
this human gone berserk, arbiter of fishscraps,
the maestro who conducted the symphony
of their hunger . . .

"Easy, Paca" croons the captain, motioning us
to close in down the larboard side; Paca's knife
triangulates snippets of fog with drops
of fishblood splattering on our faces

when a downrigger line whips from tether,
sings the salmon song, the fish rising, twisting,
something like Paca's anger against the unknown

to the skipper's anguished cry, "No—nooooooo, Paca!"
as Paca cuts the line & leader, the big fish lost
in fog & foam: all over in an instant, Paca scuffles,
subdued, tied with a bowline, hands to feet.

"That was a 38-pounder," shouts the skipper,
"Every pound comin' from your pay." Paca nods,
grins, understands as we take turns nursing him
from a bottle of Bud, the skipper untying him
before we dock, picks Paca up like a baby seal,

hands him gently over the rail to one of Paca's
many uncles who tips his fedora to the skipper.
"Adios," says the uncle, "Until five a.m.
tomorrow. Paca will face the fish, brave as any man."

SERMON FOR THE SEA LION ON BELL BUOY
NUMBER NINE

I come about
to the bell buoy's clangorous sound, sky mauve
with reddish tints of gray, landbirds becoming
blips of light on a radar screen, parishioners
visiting from shore

To see the dead sea lion,
This huge mute clapper, so inert on the platform float,
rising, falling in a vast cathedral
spun of air and foam. I see a gillnet's infectious string
strung around its throat, eyes open

To the saltwash rinse,
fierce staredown with the sun. Before I throw
the grappling iron I watch kestrels riding thermals,
as if waiting for man's words to rise
above the tolling. Then, when

The sea lion slides slowly down
to a deeper sleep, a brown pelican quickly
takes its place, turns a fish around in its great
throat pouch, showing me a flash of salmon tail
before the swallowing.

THE LADY IN RED

As soon as my grief therapist
steps into her robe, skips out
      of my head
I return to the story that keeps
      me from drinking: be it pitiful
or apocryphal, it goes something
      like this—
A young American diplomat is posted
      to South America. He goes to five
consecutive embassy parties. At the
      fifth he sees a beguiling figure
in a red dress. He asks for a dance.
      The lady says NO for three reasons:
1) You are drunk; 2) They are playing
      the Brazilian National Anthem; and
3) I am the Archbishop of Chile.
      Then, thirst assuaged, I turn over,
go back to sleep
      counting the lambs of God.

Note: *You may watch Ray reading this poem on
YouTube: Enter "Ray Clark Dickson The Lady In Red"
in the search field.*

BOOK II

Uncle Ray's RAP-sodies

The Author is 94 years old as of this writing and the poems that follow.

They are a challenge to young poets who are comfortable with, and write only, in Rap form.

Please continue your natural, refreshing style, but expand poetic reach. You'll be surprised at your universal knowledge and courageous expression.

Contemporary society is now welcoming the impactive alliteration. Ad agencies are searching for fresh Rap sounds. A state college in Arizona is awarding a minor degree in Rap. Now is the time to visit your local library. A friendly librarian will help you reach your goals in this exciting new world of the internet.

—the author

ON THE METEOR

Everything in the air is a meteor,
drop of rain, dust, snow, therefore

Man is not a meteorologist but an
astronomist, a very good man to know.

SANDBURG'S SONG

Nothing must puncture the infrastructure,
no bitter ride as genocide, deceive

The air we breathe; Karl Sandburg's
"Poet's Song," rights the wrong,

"The birth of a baby is God's way to say
the world will go on."

VEXED TEXT

Vexed by student texts?
Thought processing distressing?

Something to say for the
emotional and moral way?

Is Algebra 2 a tasteless brew,
curriculum long overdue?

A dazzling page for the Energy
Age, let brilliant young students

Set the stage?

THE PATH

Silence without violence:
On the path below my street,

Does the Western Meadowlark
have tiny spurs on its feet?

I envy the repository of shared
curiosity of what I see, a

Plumage of aristocracy, but for
a stain on my windowpane,

Reminding me of what
loneliness can be.

BIOMETRICS OF THE DAY

Everybody dies,
but not everyone lives.
—Anon.

If property, intellectual, remains in limbo, sequencing
    genes akimbo, dna out to play,
One single malt a day, beta blocker shockers,

Silky satins seeking patents, diagnostic imagery, CT
    body symmetry, a romp
For workman's comp, atomic clocks time our walks,

Sectarian or sanitarium, simple or semantic, pulsing,
    still alive? Technology deserves
Apology, nothing about you without you, if we are

To survive.

EN FAMILLE

Some say social change rides the range,
parroting high-investment parenting;

Think of the thrills in building skills
for a special hood partly understood,

Sustainable and retainable, along a
trend-line amenable, a language clipped

For hypersonic lips, and what arrives
in the archives are dancing in the astroids,

Pirouetting in the passions, all the fashions
left behind.

BADMINTON BIRDS

Arguments are badminton birds, wily, smashed
hard and slyly, over the net of political regret,

Until all run for cover, transferring answers
to another; think of Malthus, who had

A hungry mouth, predicted both rain and drought,
whatever one has sought, these birds fly
from tree to tree, sectarians follow obediently.

FAST TRAFFIC

If the mind steers through fast traffic of the
monosyllabic, why is the total anecdotal?

Back to square one: all by a career chameleon
who speeds on every road he's on, changes
color with a yawn, laments the human

Document, not to bore, but remind the top-
set its not flop-sweat, but a vector
to the public sector, asked by a woman

Called Liz, is this the way you want it to be,
or the way it is?

AUDIOPHILE

To disparage a collector's dream
is not my theme, most offer a prayer

For a MP3 player, let sound abound
day and night, car or plane, over

Clunky chunks of the melodic insane.
My collectables are riffs and tones,

Packed carefully, assiduously,
in change of homes, fine tooth combs

Of garage and attic, slow, not frantic,
waiting first for my ears alone.

A GLOW IN THE UNDERTOW

We are relieved to know what's
that glow in the undertow; sharks

Are fishflesh feeders, not survival-
eaters; groupers, striped bass, snapper,

Redfish make a tasty dish; halibut, cod
and sea bass allow the tilapia to pass;

Salmon and tuna are the leaner of white
fish, every wish, all found in Vitamin

Sea, energy for you and me.

DOROTHY AT THE ALGONQUIN

—A noted literary arts
hotel in NYC

May I present an antic touch
for the elderly who talk too much,

At the Algonquin, New York City,
rendezvous of the wise & witty,

Dorothy Parker was heard to say,
'Brevity is the soul of lingerie.'

KELPHELP

Why is kelp environment a target
for retirement, a natural disaster

For our hereafter? I see a large set
of waves searching for caves,

Rolling white flags of suffering sea
slag, one last display, a rusted model-A's key,

Backing its way for a rest near the quay.

BEACHYKLEAN

When kelp rockfish and cabejon
find it hard to carry on, nature

Teaches us to keep clean beaches,
Past the sun and moon's far reaches,

No snarly underbrush of bottled tusk,
Man's heavy lid on struggling squid,

Just a glitterland of sparkled sand
to command, beat tamba drums

And play our ukes, all night long
to sing our songs, scare way those

Watery spooks.

FRET FINGER BLUES

The sound, in a major key, declares
musical liberty; a fret finger strums

The blues, slow dancing shoes, hearts
breaking like a string on a stand-up bass,

Interface a beat profound, barely heard
on the edge of town, where curtains

Of night are slowly coming down.

JAZZ DOG MAN

He's a jazz dog man, underneath
his fur is tan, tail thumps on the beat,

Growl deserves a tweeker's tweet,
groovy kindness always sweet,

Paws scratching for a rap, shared
in the owner's lap.

OPPORTUNISTIC

Is lipstick opportunistic, or a beauty shield
that may or may not yield? Before

You kiss, remember as a teen, the short miss
on the putting green, loss of esteem,

So be careful of your tender years,
that nothing appears to cause tears, or

Disassociate romance from the field.

6.10

If the lady you admire was to acquire
a Harry Winston pure pink 6.10 ring,

Would her puzzled heart give thanks
for the offering or much more, that she

Knew you were the conspirator, love, of course,
will win, can't wait for it to begin.

A SCOLDING INNER-EAR

When a scolding inner-ear becomes clear,
the kindness of your voices is most dear,

It's like being woken after dreams have spoken,
old friends materialize before your eyes,

Mesmerize, as if an unexpected texting
relieves the vexing, and I truly am alive!

MESSAGE TREE

If the pulse of political will
becomes still from warm-up

Acts who forgot the facts, the
jagged pegs of over-regs,

Nothing wiser, no tranquilizer,
Our youth will still pin votes

On the message tree, and like
the Boston Marathon, keep

Our spirit soaring on.

POLYPHONIC

Is there a polyphonic voice, multiplicity
of choice, a tonal tribal E, triple-tongue above
high-C or a cantabile sung only to the sea?

No dragging rhythmic rancor, multi-camera
sweep, indiscrete, soccer fields of Socratic
thought, tirelessly taught, masters of

Malicious mood, subdued, subtle sensations,
humility of the heart's creations, where
all live an saliferous life, feathering beauty

In the last of light?

TIGER'S TREAD

Older men trend, near the end,
it's said, leaping with tiger's tread

To the nearest Club Med,
A warning sent in brushing

His fur on the bar where the hunt,
once afar, will begin all over again.

OBITS FOR ROBOTS

Why is there no obits for Robots
who score an abundance of chores?

Not to mention real-life contentions,
do questions, dishes, clean halls,

Malls, put sleepy heads gently in beds,
host parties for a gaggle of newly-weds,

Takes care of an intoxicated mayor,
Defends his master from disaster,

An encyclopedia of good for the social
media, a press that finally understood.

TALKING IN TIMEROUS TIMES

Is there a talking point in every coffee joint,
pro and con, everyone knows what's

Going on, perhaps this is the time, it seems,
for an alexandrine, verse of esteem,

With six iambic ft. whose length alone
may well condone theatrics of our theme.

STREAMLINES

As if we can't forget, we hear
live streams on internet, brows wet

From cultured screams, as if the
ceremonious are harmonious,

And when all bold tales are told,
the significant remains in dreams.

SAT NUMEROS

Do numbers numb the intellect,
respect or disrespect a skill,

Will SAT sit still for a 1600 thrill,
Kids allowed a brilliant tiny

Spill, or by a capricious shill
whose count only pays the bill?

CLASS ACT

Please don't foment an anxious moment,
heed the base-line of your bathos,

Liquidity of your tears, whisper goodbye
as equanimity disappears; Pass crystals

On the table, drugs disable, cannibalize
your cravings, eliminate savings,

Finalize your fate, end in a 6x8 with
heavy freight; So remember to remember,

The code of conduct is true splendor,
hear the people say, he or she is a

Class Act, everyday!

PEDRO'S PASSION

Pedro Calderon de la Barca
Stenciled wisdom on his parka,

A Spanish dramatist of the 1600s
Would explain our social blunders,

Dear loving dove, "When love is
not madness, it is not love."

THE NBA FOR KIDS TODAY

Something good to know, just say
Uncle Ray told me so: The NBA

Finds energy in buildings? Things
like pick and roll extols the physical,

Not whimsical, Suspense? Winners
in defense? A tantalizing tort

Executes in half-court? Do referees
sob and bawl a human-nature call?

Is pro life's rowel a technical or
personal foul? Is the last shot

A clock shot or the game shot?
Finally, besides fission, there must

Be a heartbeat in transmission.

CAVEAT

Is a caveat a forget-me-not of Soul,
Folk, Country Rock? Drones

Delivering scones at 700' above the
metronome? Remembering her face,

Chantilly Lace, lips, at first blush,
waiting in the dusk?

SOCIOLOGY I

He speaks California cell-phone lingua,
A monotone filling all strong ears—

Wears a peak-bill cap, New Orleans Yard Dog,
Green silk croc embossed on brim—

The Caesar hairstyle abuts Crew Cut,
Long abandoned Buzz-Top between—

Autographs sweat towels for buddies
At the gym; carries a Nikon Coolpix 5,000.

Snaps everyone & everything before
He lets the day begin.

WOODSWORTHIAN

Uncle Ray's proud in what you do,
bringing rap up a notch or two,

Our cool plan will sweep the land,
becomes a true Woodsworthian.

LANGUISHING LOSER

A man, emasculated by loss of wealth,
still too smart for stealth, drives around

The bank at night, waves at all gendarmes
in sight, so, mired in chronic economics

Welcomes the first of light.

SOCIAL STORM

Those hurt in a shameful social
storm can still perform

Life's vital role, remembering
love's agenda pacifies

The soul.

For nine decades, Ray Clark Dickson, born in Portland, Oregon, 1919, has written with clarity, sensitivity and narrative power. A state track champion, Ray won an athletic scholarship to the University of Oregon, graduating with a degree in journalism. An experienced drummer, he formed and led his own 12-piece Big Band, performed during university years and on the road. During World War Two, Ray served in the Pacific Theatre as a Captain in the Marine Corps.

In his youth, Ray worked in Oregon sawmills and at coastal ports, absorbing revelations of mountains, the sea, and people he met. He spent a year in Mexico writing narrative poetry and pulp fiction novels during Jack Kerouac's time there in 1952. Widely traveled, he is noted for volatility and resonance of language, fusing traditional forms into street and jazz poetry, and applying antic and complex structures at different levels. First published at nine years of age, Ray has covered most of the 20th century, and now into the 21st continues with Bergson's concept of Durée, 'We carry with us all our rolling experience compacted in the ever-growing snowball of our lives.'

Ray has published hundreds of poems, including 22 in the highly noted *Beloit Poetry Journal.* He was selected for Beloit's Anthology *A Fine Excess: Fifty Years Of The Beloit Poetry Journal (2000),* along with inspirational mentors, William Carlos Williams, Galway Kinnell, Philip Levine, Gwendolyn Brooks and others. He has a CD, *Cocoloba,* background à la Cuba jazz. A publisher's proof of his sixth chapbook, *The San Francisco Pit Band Blues*, was requested by UCLA's Special Collection, Poetry Archives. *The Press Corps of Xanadu,* was published by iUniverse in 2007. *Wingbeats After Dark,* Red Hen Press, Los Angeles, 2009, was his tenth book of poetry. *With the Blood of Butterflies,* his eleventh book, was published by Infinity Press in 2011. *Parlando II* is his twelfth book and published by iUniverse in 2014. Note: iUniverse was recently acquired by Penguin Random House.

Ray was chosen as the First Poet Laureate, city and county, San Luis Obispo, 1999, and nominee by the San Luis Obispo Arts Council for State Poet Laureate, 2002.

He lives in San Luis Obispo with his wife of 30 years, Marysia Maziarz, author of Polish-American fiction.